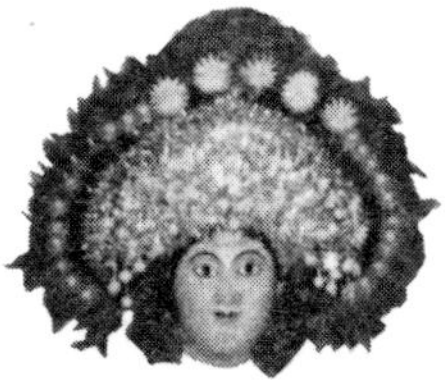

WRITING IDENTITIES

Folklore and Performative Arts of Purulia, Bengal

WRITING IDENTITIES
Folklore and Performative Arts of Purulia, Bengal

ROMA CHATTERJI

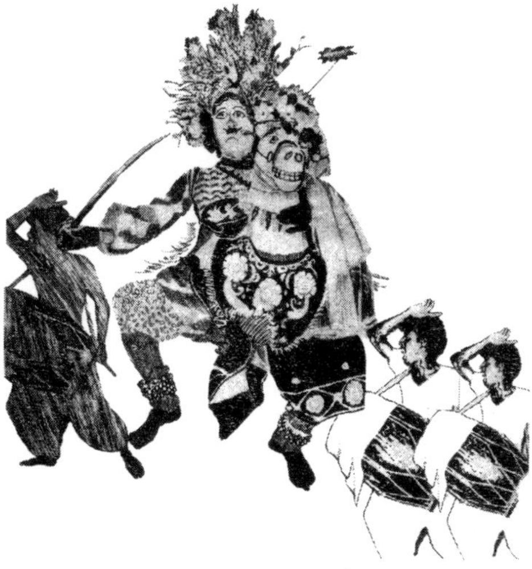

INDIRA GANDHI NATIONAL CENTRE
FOR THE ARTS
New Delhi

ARYAN BOOKS INTERNATIONAL
New Delhi

WRITING IDENTITIES
Folklore and Performative Arts of Purulia, Bengal

ISBN: 978-81-7305-378-8

Published in **2009** by

INDIRA GANDHI NATIONAL CENTRE FOR THE ARTS
Janpath, New Delhi-110 001 (India)
and
ARYAN BOOKS INTERNATIONAL
Pooja Apartments, 4B, Ansari Road, New Delhi-110 002 (India)
Tel.: 23287589, 23255799; Fax: 91-11-23270385
E-mail: aryanbooks@vsnl.com, aryanbooks@gmail.com

Computer Typeset and Printed in India at
ABI Prints & Publishing Co., New Delhi.

The Indira Gandhi National Centre for the Arts (IGNCA) is actively engaged in research, documentation, publication and dissemination of knowledge about folk culture. As contemporary traditions, the IGNCA, especially through its programmes under the Janapada Sampada, recognises that forms of folk culture are embedded in social life. When social institutions change, some folk forms are able to adapt to new conditions of existence but others are not so fortunate. One of the expressed aims of the IGNCA is to try and sustain all forms of folk culture not by preserving them as specimens in a museum but rather by supporting the institutions that could best allow their articulation. To this end, the Janapada Sampada, as the division directly concerned with the diverse forms of India's folk culture, is actively engaged in re-establishing these traditions in their socio-economic context and in disseminating knowledge about their role in shaping Indian society and culture.

Foreword

Chhó dance, Jhumur songs, Bhadu *puja* in Purulia have served as platforms in this volume for a historiographic exploration of folklore studies and performances in West Bengal, Bihar and Jharkhand. The exploration situates itself in the history of the passage of oral into print culture. It speaks of the use of folklore for political, social, economic or intellectual movements. It shows how folk art has been harnessed to objectives of strengthening feudal hierarchy, promoting social ascent, boosting national or regional self esteem, or ensuring appropriation of orality in self reflective intellectual or semiotic discourse. It also reveals the tremendous energy of folk art forms that have enabled them to survive and recharge themselves, like Antaeus drawing strength from the earth.

The discourse is an embattled arena, agog with the babble of voices. There are strident protests about tribal folklore being taken over by non-tribals. The tribal voice of Gambhir Singh Mura is reported to have been misappropriated by a castest political agenda according to scholars such as Pashupati Mahato, a self-professed tribal scholar. A tribal agricultural festival is alleged to have been colonized by Hindu rajas of Kashipur for encouraging the planting of *bhadui dhan* or the post monsoon paddy harvest. Tribal personifications of forces of nature have been expropriated for presenting Hindu Gods and Goddesses. Worship of Siva has been substituted for worship of the Sun. Rain making rituals of the Dom infantry of the local chieftain has been exploited in the ritual calendar to avoid rebellion according to the influential folklorist Ashutosh Bhattacharya. Primitive Christian, ethical, non-anthropomorphic or Promethean elements have been transplanted in Munda religion and origin myths, in an attempt to domesticate tribal folklore in Christian religion as exemplified in the works of Hoffman and Van Exem. Pantheistic elements in the Baha festival have been misread for domestication in global environmentalism.

If there are allegations about misuse of tribal folklore for extraneous objectives, tribal voices have been raised to claim affinity with non-tribal society in an urge for Rajputization or Sanskritization. Bhumijas in Birbhum, according to N.K. Bose, have claimed kinship with the Bagmundi rajas. Siva has been viewed as Kirata, a tribal hunter, leading to the use of Purulia chhó in films by Ritwik Ghatak, and Kshatriya status has been asserted by Kurmi Mahatos in the Jharkhand census. Radha-Krishna have been metamorphosed into a tribal couple in Jharkhand.

In a further ramification of the discourse, the following suggestions have been made about the politics of cultural nationalism. Tribal and folk dance has been incorporated in the Sahaja-Swadeshi synthesis of Gurusaday Dutt's Bratachari *melas*. The IPTA has harnessed folk songs to socialist realism in histrionics on the Bengal famine of 1943. Coomaraswamy has reconstituted folklore as sacred, *marga* and classicist, in reaction against colonial, orientalist construction.

A resurgence of regional, sub-regional and primordial identities has been counter posed against the reassertion of cultural nationalism. The Tushu satyagraha of the early sixties, has united Muslim and Hindu peasants, in a demand for integration of Purulia with Bengal rather than Bihar. The Dom is the Pashan *jati* in the Sharaboli text or the *bhumij jati* in Gambhir Singh Mura's village Chorida as interpreted by the choreographer of his Chhó dance troupe, Anil Shutradhar. Mahasveta Devi says that the Shabara oral tradition has been resuscitated on the foundation of epics such as the *Mangala Kavyas* and novelists such as Nilankatha Ghoshal have constructed characters such as Bhumi Kanya on the basis of Bhadu myths.

There is a substratum of gender reconstruction of history. The feminine has been suggested as the other in a gender oblivious, revivalist Hinduism. Bhadu is a woman, transformed into a Goddess, on death. Radha's identity is submerged in Jhumur, a male preserve. Authoritative, patriarchal structures are subverted by breaking conjugal silence, imposed by society in proscribed songs. The feminine voice of Sati, Parvati or Sita has been quoted as one of doubt and interrogation.

Transcending the printed work of individual folklorists, folklore institutions, or folklore journals like *Chhatrak* and *Lokshruti* and the cacophony of debating voices, raises the unmistakable voice of the people. Brahmins and Bhats perform rituals, Shutradhars make chhó masks and Doms and Ghasis make music and mingle their voices in symphony. Kobywala competitions, Khemta or Jhumurwali dances, Hanka, Gaha, Bhaduria, Dandshalya, Nachnishalya dances are performed in step with the rhythm of seasons, work and festivals, Jharkhandi *kirtan* and Vishnupuri *gharana*, courtly and rural styles, *deshi* and *margi* genres come together in an orchestra. Sensual and spiritual elements, egalitarian and exploitative approaches, narrative and spectacular presentations, Gods, animals and human beings, Muslim, Buddhist, Brahmin and tribal ethnoses, primordial and contemporary imagination, converge filmi and folk music. The polyphonic mix of *bhavas, layas*, drum beats; exaggerated *chala* gestures, threaded with the colourful iconography and dramatic succession of characters; the breathless build up and denouement – these are the vital pulsations that come out inexorably through the maze and weave of debates. *Katha* and *Kahani*, history and story join hands. The poignant narrative of the death of Bhadu, the princess, the stark detail in Jhumur songs on Bon Jhara *akal* or forest famine, hits us hard. The intimate, personal involvement of Parvati with her worshipper, or the death of Sati, in a question mark on the authority of Siva and Daksha, wring our heart strings.

The hierophantic presentation of myth as part of reality, the paratactic chain tying domestic and public events in a ritual space, use of social imaginary and cultural alterity as part of a contested territory between universal and local values, the incorporation of a new aesthetics in the public domain through folklore studies, or the folk critique of bhadralok society are elements of the discourse, that recede into the background. We stop and listen to the poetic and musical voice of the people of Purulia, regale ourselves with the spectacle staged by them, and vibrate with the gamut of emotions traversed by them in their cultivated but frenetic movements.

K.K. Chakravarty

Preface

I researched the folklore of Purulia in the early 1980s as a Ph.D. student from Delhi University. The choice of subject and location were partly determined by the paucity of literature on this field and partly from the fact that my department laid great emphasis on the fieldwork tradition. Apart from a few intrepid geographers and some folklorists who wrote in Bangla, Purulia was virtually unknown in the scholarly literature. This was so in spite of a vibrant tradition of debate via the print media within Purulia itself. I realized within the first few months of fieldwork that I could not treat my field location as an isolated face-to-face community within a predominately oral tradition. It was a centre of discourse that encompassed not only other local traditions in the wider cultural region of Jharkhand and Bengal but also a print culture that was using folklore as a site on which to reflect upon itself. The biannual journal *Chhatrak* edited by Professor Subodh Bosu Roy of J. K. College, Purulia, became the forum through which Purulia itself could be thematised as an object of study.

Fifteen years later, when I re-visited the field in 1999 I realised that Purulia was no longer considered marginal to the intellectual discourse in Bengal. I found a wealth of literature on the folklore and culture of Purulia, written in Bangla and published largely by the Government of West Bengal. What brought about this new interest in Purulia? It is this question that provided the initial impetus for my work. At first sight it would seem that government policy and the cultural politics of the region were being thematised in the print culture here. A closer reading of the published material however, does not reveal a one-to-one connection between the two. There is a remarkable continuity in the way that Purulia is presented in these works – from the early writings of Ashutosh Bhattacharya, one of the first scholars to write about the folklore of Purulia in the 1960s and 1970s to more recent folkloric accounts. What accounts for this representational stability? I argue that it is the discourse of folklore that is largely responsible for this fact. It is Foucault who first said that discourse creates its own "pre-existing forms of continuity" – a synthesis based on the "already said" (1972:25). I would extend this further to say that "communities of discourse" such as those constituted by folklorists, are created through the selection not so much of modes of representation but rather of the expressive genres themselves. Thus folklore, at least Bengali folklore can be thought of as constituting a genre in itself.

Bakhtin (1986) broadens the concept of genre to include everyday forms of utterance, saying that the specific contexts in which language is used develop stable genres of speech. The focus on genre foregrounds the sensitivity of language to context as well as to the intentions of the users, in that speakers actively choose the genres in which they wish to couch their utterances. Bakhtin's formulation focuses on the ideological standpoint of the addresser – on his or her work plan reflected in the choice of genre. But equally it is the choice of audience, the addressee one hopes to reach out to that forms a potential community of discourse.

Contemporary scholars like Flueckiger (1994, 1996) have made creative use of folklore genres to problematise the notion of 'community'. Writing about Chhatisgarhi folklore she says that there is a strong identification between genre and community. This principle, in fact, underpins the indigenous performative system. In my previous work on the performative tradition of Purulia, I found that even though indigenous classifications of folklore genres tend to privilege links with groupings based on caste and gender, there are also some cases of cultural transgression. Thus women, for instance, sometimes compose and sing in genres of songs that are proscribed according to tradition (Chatterji 1987, 2002). In this volume my interest in genre is of a somewhat different order. I show how Bangla folkloristics first presents Purulia as a cultural region through the description of certain performative genres and then constitutes these genres as boundary markers. Thus the choice of genre for description delineates 'community' in a certain way. The performative genres that are the objects of folkloric discourse become the prisms through which the 'folk community' is constituted. I do not mean to imply that this community is presented as a seamless whole. Rather each genre that is described presents the community in a way that is singular and different from its presentation through the lens of the other genres.

I examine folklore writings on three important genres, viz. the *chhó* dance, the *jhūmūr* song and the myths and songs associated with the Bhadu ritual (*pūjā*), to describe some of the ways in which community comes to be represented in Purulia. My selection is based on the fact that these are the genres most often used to constitute specific representations of community life. Interestingly, these are also the genres that have been the subject of institutional forms of patronage for a considerable period of time – a fact of some importance for the print culture of Purulia.

Let me now give an account of some of the institutions and activities that have shaped the ways in which Purulia is represented in the print culture. Institutionalised forms of patronage have a significant role to play in the development and stabilisation of the idea of culture as an isolable sphere. In this work I describe this process in terms of two systems of patronage, that is, the government bureaucracy, in the post-Independence period and the feudal courts that emerged in Purulia about two hundred years ago (Sinha 1995). Both systems have had seminal influence in giving shape to the three performative genres that I have mentioned.

THE FOLKLORISATION OF CULTURE: 'THE FOLK AND TRIBAL CULTURAL CENTRE'

The Folk and Tribal Cultural Centre of the Government of West Bengal was established in the early 1980s for the promotion and publication of research on the folk culture of West Bengal. In an interview, Professor Mihir Bhattacharya, who has been associated with this centre since its inception, told me that the first attempts at establishing government institutions for the preservation and study of folk culture began in the late 1970s. An advisory committee called the *Loksanskriti Parishad* (Folk Culture Committee) was set up to explore possibilities of district level interaction. Members of this committee organised workshops in the different districts of West Bengal to facilitate interaction between folk artists, local scholars and government agencies. By the late eighties, the district level bodies were sufficiently 'sensitised', to use Professor Bhattacharya's words, to organise and fund their own local assemblies with local artists and with the help of local *panchayats*. The government also set up a series of awards for folk artists and has instituted scholarships and pension schemes for folk performers. *Lokshruti*, the biannual journal brought out by the Centre, has become an important forum for intellectual debate and reflection on the folk culture of West Bengal.

The significance of such forms of government intervention lies in the fact that it creates sites on which a new form of local self-knowledge can emerge. Most of the scholars who contribute to *Lokshruti* have a moral and political stake in the constitution of folk culture itself. For them, folk culture embodies the symbolic imaginary through which they can critique certain trends in *bhadralok* society. Folklore then represents the site which is both *of* Bengali society and yet not fully *in* it. The folk become a virtual community used to delineate the spiritual qualities not just of the region, but also through the mediation of state agencies, of the nation itself (Dutt 1990).

Clearly government intervention in folk culture has allowed the latter to be transposed on a different register such that it can be co-opted by new forms of institutionalisation. The print media is one such form. Since Anderson's (1983) seminal work, its role in the articulation of new political entities has been extensively studied. In India, forms of folk culture have been re-articulated by print media in the service of new political formations (Ashley 1993). In the process they also acquire a new kind of aesthetic autonomy such that can absorb new contexts of performance. It is often assumed by folklorists that state intervention is the sole agent responsible for the aestheticisation[1] of folk culture. However folk societies are usually part of larger political formations that have over time led to the transformation of folk culture (Rappaport 1994). In Purulia, as this volume will show, the performative genres that have lent themselves to appropriation by the print culture had already undergone a process of aestheticisation in the courts of the feudal chiefs in this region and have been successfully reincorporated into the folk communities in which they originally took shape. In Purulia, at least, as I will show, an impulse towards aesthetic autonomy was already present in the folk society.

STATE FORMATION IN TRIBAL CENTRAL INDIA

Purulia was part of the Jungle Mahals – the hill areas that ranged from Birbhum, now in the state of West Bengal to Ranchi, now in Jharkhand – until this district was dissolved in 1833. It then became part of the district of Manbhum in Bihar. Manbhum, in turn, was dissolved in 1956 and Purulia became a separate district in the state of West Bengal. It still has strong cultural links with the state of Jharkhand, which was carved out of Bihar a few years ago.

The tribal belt of Central India, of which Purulia forms a part, is of great significance for understanding the process by which the aestheticisation of folk culture takes place.[2] Surajit Sinha (1995) is one of the few scholars in India who has discussed the relationship between the agricultural tribes of Central India with feudalistic institutions of the state – a process that he calls the 'Rajputisation' of the tribes. This refers to the development of an aristocratic stratum within the tribes of this region. He does not discuss the influence of this process on tribal culture per se but it is probable that the process of Rajputisation went hand-in-hand with the emergence of a regional courtly culture (Bhattacharya 1986). The courts of the tribal chiefs or *zamindārs* were important centres of patronage where performers and poets congregated. It is important to remember that the forms that became the object of royal patronage were folk forms, such as the *chhó* dance and *jhūmūr* song and so on. Thus local styles of music and dance developed in these courts. Bagmundi, a relatively small *zamindāri* of eighty three *mouzas* (revenue villages) developed its own style of rendering the *jhūmūr* that is called the *Bāgmuṇḍyā* and was able to attract the best dancers and *jhūmūr* singers to its court (Bhattacharya 1986). However, the links with folk culture were never severed and even today, when the tribal *zamindārs* have disappeared, the musical tradition that they nurtured has become, as it always was, the heritage of the folk. In my opinion, it is precisely those forms that had already acquired an autonomous aesthetic through royal patronage that lend themselves most readily to outside intervention. Thus, the *chhó* dance has adapted to new performative contexts in such a way that its popularity is enhanced in its own regional base. This has not happened with the *nāṭuā* dance, for instance. It does not travel well and its popularity at home has declined. The *chhó* developed into a form of high art in Bagmundi, the *nāṭuā* did not, even though stylistically they are very similar.

The village Chorida, where I lived for a year and a half, was inhabited by groups of service and artisan castes that had been settled there by the *rājā* to serve the Bagmundi court. Brahmins and Bhatts performed the court rituals and the Shutradhars made masks for the *chhó* dance and sacred images of Bhadu for the annual Bhadu *pūjā*.[3] Doms and Ghasis served as court musicians. Some families of Bhumij, who are thought to be the original inhabitants of Chorida, claimed kinship with the Bagmundi *rājās*. They said that the *rājā's* lineage had diverged from their own three generations previous to the present generation, when the *rājās* had become "Kshatriya" and began to intermarry only with other Kshatriyas (see also Sinha 1995). The simultaneous articulation of two cultural registers – tribal and caste Hindu – in the expression of Bhumij identity is also reflected in the domain of aesthetics as I have just said. It also means that categories such as folk and classical must not be seen as mutually exclusive. Musical genres like the *jhūmūr* can be heard as both folk as well as classical depending on the particular form of sociality within which they are thought to be embedded.

How are different forms of sociality to be addressed anthropologically? What are the kinds of representation within which they can be anchored? In the last section I examine the space of discourse and the constitution of the public as the space within which such questions can be posed.

THE AESTHETIC PRINCIPLE AND THE DEVELOPMENT OF THE PUBLIC

How is the establishment of an autonomous aesthetic principle related to the modern discourse of folklore and the transformation of folk culture? Once these cultural forms begin to be thought of as autonomous entities, they become free to circulate in other spheres and become incorporated within other forms of sociality. These new forms of sociality could be thought of as publics constituted through the circulation of discourse itself (Warner 2002). I think of the institution of folklore studies in West Bengal as contributing to the development of such a public. The discourse of folklore co-exists with the folk traditions that it supposedly represents and in the process impinges on the forms themselves.

Folk culture no longer thought to be embedded exclusively in tradition. Through the intervention of folklore studies, it has become part of the public domain and in a sense contemporaneous with more modern forms of culture. This is reflected in the writings that I discuss here. There is an attempt, in these writings, to break away from the representation of folk culture as being embedded in an idyllic and timeless face-to-face community and link forms of folk culture to contemporary assertions of identity and belonging. However, in the process, these forms become essentialised in new ways, as I will show. In the first three chapters, I show how a set of discourses selectively constitutes a specific cultural form as an iconic representation of the 'folk' or 'tribe'. Each one of these forms is used to represent a particular dimension of folk culture such that they seem to function as a set of sliding frames within which contradictory aspects of 'folk' culture are successively foreground. In each of these chapters, I juxtapose these representations with ethnographic description culled from my field notes written in the 1980s. By doing so I hope to demonstrate that it is only in the concatenation of different voices that a more complex picture of folk society will emerge.

The particular representations of folk or tribe that are foregrounded in the descriptions of these forms also have to do with a larger thematic, that is, of Purulia as a cultural region. As I have shown in a previous work Bangla folklore scholarship, supported by state policy, has created a discursive field in which the category of folk is used to conceptualise a region. (Chatterji 2005, 2003). The historical process by which particular areas come to be perceived as folklore regions is an issue that I will briefly touch upon in the concluding chapter. Suffice it to say here that in Bengal folklore continues to have an important ideological role in the articulation of regional identity. Academic writings on folk culture have also emphasised the conception of 'cultural region' as a source of folklore's engagement with modernity (Morinis 1982, Blackburn 2003). It is precisely at this level that self-conscious reflection on context, style and the process of transmission actually occurs. This is the place at which the local is conceived off as such and thus also the point at which "metadiscursive practices for creating, representing and interpreting" folk discourses are developed (Briggs 1993).

The last chapter is, stylistically speaking, in a different key – it discusses the subversive potential of the feminine voice and its significance for our understanding of folk culture in general. I have included it in this collection to foreground the problematical relationship between individual voices in the field and the representations of tradition that we produce through our scholarly writings. By showing the dialogical potential within folklore genres themselves I wish to problematise the way in which the notion of collective voice is presented as a given in most writings on folklore and the oral tradition. Instead, I argue that spaces of individual self-reflection are already available within the traditional folk genres themselves, so that the 'new' modes of reflection provided by folklore studies can be accommodated within these spaces without much dislocation.

Finally, in conclusion, I examine the ideas of some important nationalists whose writings have had a seminal influence on the development of folklore studies in Bengal. Even though their work has no direct bearing on Purulia (most of the important folklore collections before independence were carried out in East Bengal), it has influenced the way in which Purulia is conceptualised as a folkloric region. I also contrast this genre of folklore writing with another body of writing that has emerged from the Catholic church based in Chota Nagpur, on the assumption that the silences within a particular kind of discourse can only be foregrounded through a juxtaposition with a discourse that is entirely different.

NOTES

1. By 'aestheticisation' I mean the process by which an independent measure of evaluation is developed for cultural forms like dance and music, outside the context of participation usually associated with folk forms.
2. The development of an autonomous aesthetic domain in folk culture may help in resisting the 'folklorisation' of folk culture.
3. In fact one of the Shutradhar families in Chorida still lives on the *Bhadu bāṛi* (Bhadu house), that is land that was given by the chief for making the royal Bhadu image every year.

Contents

Acknowledgements

This book has been a long time in the making and there are many people who have contributed to it. I must begin by thanking the Member Secretary, Dr. K.K. Chakravarty of the Indira Gandhi National Centre for the Arts whose support made this project possible. I also express by deep gratitude to Prof. Jyotindra Jain and Ms. Aditi Mehta for their support and co-operation. I owe a special debt of gratitude to my friend Molly Kaushal and the staff of the Janapada Sampada. Molly was instrumental in bringing this work to fruition and the staff of the Janapada Sampada have helped with the administrative details that I did not always understand. Veena Das, Deepak Mehta, Mani Shekhar Singh, J.V. Meenakshi and Rimli Bhattacharya have all been generous with their time. Over the years the discussions that I have had with them have been invaluable. Ranen Das has always been available for support and advice. In Calcutta conversations with, Mihir Bhattacharya, Divyajyoti Mazumdar and Pashupati Mahato have helped to crystallise many of the issues discussed here. Abhijit Dasgupta gave me my first introduction to the print culture of Calcutta. Lectures and presentations at the departments of English and Modern Indian Languages, Delhi University, the department of Linguistics and Literature, Jawaharlal Nehru University, and the department of Anthropology, University of California at Berkeley helped me to clarify the ideas presented here. I must thank Charles Briggs, Dorothy Noyes, Lawrence Cohen, Manju Jain, Sadhana Naithani and P. Patnaik for inviting me to share my ideas with their colleagues and students. Mr. Golok Sarkar came with me to Chorida village and took the photographs reproduced here. My parents, grandparents and relatives in Calcutta have been a source of encouragement from the very first time I set foot in Purulia. I owe a debt of gratitude to Ivy and Nataraj Chatterji, Manushi, Kamalika and Shagarika Lahiri, Monotosh Mukherjee, Sambhit Chatterjee, Saumitra and Deepa Chatterjee. Finally, apart from the staff of the IGNCA, I must also acknowledge the support of the research and administrative staff of both the Institute for Socio-Economic Research on Development and Democracy, Delhi and the Folk and Tribal Cultural Centre, Calcutta without whose help this work would not have been undertaken.

Note on Transliteration

All Bangla words are spelled phonetically, except for words that are well known in their Sanskritic variants. I have not used diacritical marks for proper nouns, which have been spelled as they are commonly pronounced. Proper nouns in the Bangla songs have however, been given diacritical marks to indicate correct pronunciation. I have used Bangla versions of the names of important deities only in the songs.

All Indian words are in italics.

1

The Chhó Dance and the Public Sphere

The *chhó*[1] dance of Purulia was 'discovered' in the late 1960s by Ashutosh Bhattacharya. He has described his first experience of the dance and the way in which he brought it to the attention of the outside world in many of his writings. The following excerpt is taken from the introduction to a publicity pamphlet that contains the reviews of the dance performances held in the USA in 1975.

> It has been my practice and hobby for many years past to visit the most interior parts of villages of Bengal in search of original materials for the study of folk-literature of Bengal. In 1961 I visited Purulia. Only a few years back the district of Purulia was formed with the Bengali-speaking population of the now-defunct district of Manbhum and was joined with the state of West Bengal on a linguistic and cultural basis. It was summer time and during the night I heard the beat of drums coming from all directions. I was told that a dance known as chhau dance was performed during this season and the beating of drums showed that the dance was being held everywhere in the villages with the accompaniment of its usual music. At midnight I with a batch of my students arrived at a village where the dance was in progress and I was immediately surprised by its novelty. Thenceforward, I devoted my field study to this novel form of dance hitherto unknown to the world outside.

> I attracted the notice of the Sangeet Natak Akademi, New Delhi – to this form of dance. It took immediate interest and invited me to give performances of the dance in New Delhi. In June 1969, I visited New Delhi with a batch of 40 village artists for the first time outside their native district. Performances were held there before very distinguished Indian and foreign invitees in the open lawn of Rabindra Bhavan in New Delhi. Performances were also shown in T.V. in Delhi. (Only three years later it was also shown in B.B.C. television in London and five years later in New York U.S.A.)
>
> At the encouragement of the Sangeet Natak Akademi, New Delhi, arrangement was also made for training of some artists at their villages. Since then the annual Chhau Festival in Purulia during the middle of April has become a regular feature. Even Smt. Indira Gandhi, the Prime Minister of India, has taken interest in the Annual Festival. It has been attended so far by a number of foreign dance-critics from almost every part of the world. Due mainly to their interest in the dance, invitations also come from far off countries.

(Bhattacharya 1975: 2-3)

Since this was written, the 'Chhó Dance of Purulia' has become a symbol of West Bengal's tribal Other – performed in all kinds of public forums, portrayed in literary and art works.[2] In this chapter I shall explore some of the discourses in which the *chhó* is inscribed and describe the ways in which these discourses also build notions of 'tribe' into the dance itself.

PURULIA CHHÓ AND AUTHENTIC TRADITION

Three different types of discourses have emerged around the dance in recent years – academic, activist and performative. Each of these strives to constitute a particular tradition in which to embed the dance and thus give its form a certain 'authenticity'. First, for scholars like Ashutosh Bhattacharya, the doyen of folklore studies in Bengal, the 'aboriginal' culture of Purulia is still visible beneath the thin veil of Hinduism. He tries to prove that the *chhó* is essentially a tribal war dance that acquired a Hindu veneer when it came under the patronage of the local chieftains who had themselves only recently been Sanskritised. Other scholars, taking issue with the condescending tone of Bhattacharya's writings, do not differ from him on the basic framework within which the dance is placed. Thus they also characterize the dance as tribal and magical and like Bhattacharya, they assume homogeneity in the cultural forms found in the tribes of Jharkhand with which Purulia has affinity. However, as distinct from Bhattacharya they treat tribal culture as superior to the Hinduisation that the dance has undergone. Much of this writing pre-dates the formation of the state of Jharkhand so that the latter is seen as a cultural rather than a political entity (Mahato 1978). Interestingly, some recent articles published from Calcutta locate the dance within an alternative Bengali tradition that seeks to establish a continuum between an ancient pan-Indian shastric tradition and a *deśī*, regional or folk tradition that by-passes both the medieval as well as the colonial period of Bengal's history (Roychaudhury 1996).

The search for the 'authentic tradition' of the dance by folklorists, is based on the notion of an original source. This leads to a division between the essential tribal aspect of the dance located in the music and the pattern of movements and the later accretions, that is, the narrative themes that are the subjects of the performances. The latter are thought to be a result of the slow process of acculturation that took place when these tribal groups came into contact with Hindu culture. For the dancers with whom I interacted in the course of my fieldwork there was no such dichotomy, for though they conceded that the form of the dance has altered to include narratives from the sacred Hindu texts, they considered the musical tradition on which this dance is based to have its source in these texts. For example, the late Gambhir Singh Mura, one of the most renowned exponents of Purulia *chhó*, told me that it was only the *shastras* (sacred texts) that revealed the *rasa* (flavour), *tāla* (rhythm), *chāla* (gait, movement) and *bhóṇgi* (style) of the dance. It is not accidental that one of the recent articles that seeks to locate the fragments of a lost tradition of classical dance in Bengal, is based on intensive interviews with Gambhir Singh Mura. However, Gambhir Singh never resisted outside influences if they were compatible with the mood of the themes that he danced. Whereas for scholars of folklore the question of authenticity of the dance is tied up with its 'original' form, for the dancers themselves, the dance is continuously evolving.

THE DANCE PERFORMANCE

The *chhó* is a 'folk' dance, that is, it belongs to a tradition that is not elaborately codified. The performance has been described as having a particular episodic structure: the introduction of each character in sequence, the build up to the battle, the battle and the victory dance (Natih 1985). While this may describe the sequence in which the dance episode unfolds, it does not do justice to the polyphonic nature of the performance. What the dance seeks to do is not so much narrate a story that already exists in different forms in other texts, but to present a series of images that are strung together by the music. The dancers wear masks that portray the dominant moods of the characters they are supposed to represent. The masks of the gods (*dévas*) are painted in pastel shades and have features that are delicately modelled showing expressions that are serene or benign. The masks of the demons (*asuras*) have bulging eyes and snarling lips and are painted in colours that are darker than those representing the gods. The hand gestures used by the dancers are natural though exaggerated. They do not express the moods (*bhāva*) of the characters. This is done in terms of the styles of movement displayed through the torso, the legs and the arms. Some of the important styles of movement that portray the major characters are as follows:

The heroic gait (*bīr chāla*)[3] in which the dancer takes rapid steps in a half crouched position, interspersed with high leaps, somersaults (both movements are referred to by the same term, *ulfā*) and rotations on one heal (*eḍi ghórā*). The great gods like Shiva, Durga and Kali are portrayed through the *déb chāla* (the gait of the gods). In comparison with the former gait there is far less emphasis on movement in this one. The dancers enter the dance arena with a stately shuffle and take up statuesque poses modelled on the iconography associated with temple images. There are also various animal gaits, for example, the *bāndór chāla* or monkey gait. The dancer moves with a half crouching, elongated step, legs stretched out, and arms pushed away from the body and bent at the elbows. The torso juts forward and moves to incorporate the movement of the tail that is attached to the waist, into the dance. This is a difficult gait to perform. The dancer must convey a disjointed grace and yet his movements must not be jerky. This gait is also associated with the comic mood.

Each of these gaits is associated with a character type and a dance episode will always portray a set of such character types so that there is an interweaving of different styles of movement. The characters are classified on the basis of the moods (*bhāva* or *bhaab*) they embody. These are largely the heroic, the godly and the comic as we have shown.

A character type is not continuous with the personalities found in the sacred narratives. These personalities may display a number of conflicting moods, which may be displayed in different episodes of the dance. Thus Lord Shiva, a great god, is visually portrayed through the godly gait except in one episode in which he is disguised as a hunter, and performs the heroic gait. Although the audience is familiar with the entire corpus of narratives in which Shiva is portrayed as a god, the use of the heroic gait marks out a particular moment in this corpus in which Shiva disguised himself as a hunter in order to test Arjuna, one of the heroes of the *Mahabharata*. The point is that the audience knows before hand that at the end of the narrative, the disguised hunter will reveal himself as Shiva, but the dance must portray the character that Lord Shiva adopts for this particular episode rather than portray his godly character which is known to all. Similarly there are demons who are portrayed in the heroic style. In some cases demonic characters may embody the comic type when they bear some resemblance to the animal characters in the disjointed style of their movement.

The instruments used as accompaniments for the dance are as follows:

The *ḍhol*, a barrel shaped drum played with the palm of the left hand and a stick held in the right. There are usually two *ḍhols* in a particular dance episode. They lead the dancers and there is a conversation between the *ḍhols* and the dancers.

The *dhamśā* or *nāgṛā*, a huge bowl shaped kettle drum played with two heavy and blunt sticks. The *dhāmśā* has a deep and throbbing sound.

The *śainā* or *shahnai*, a wind instrument with a high wailing sound.

The basic rhythm (*tāla*) for the dancers is provided by the *ḍhols*. The rhythm cycle is usually composed of a pattern of four beats grouped into sections of two. The tempo (*laya*) varies in the different phases of the performance. The *śainā* provides the melody (*sura* or *ṣūr*). It is usually played in the pauses that signal a movement in the narrative – either the exit of one character and the entrance of another or a shift to another phase of the story being enacted. Since no stage sets are used in the performance, shifts in location are marked by a slight pause in the dance that is filled up by the music of the *śainā*. The *dhamśā* is used only at certain moments in the performance – during the battle scene or during moments of dramatic climax.

These are the instruments that have traditionally accompanied the *chhó* dance. There are some others that have been added in more recent times such as the *kaurneṭ* or clarinet. This instrument can produce a soft rippling note and is sometimes used to create suspense in the pauses between particular dance sequences. There is also the *bañṣi* or flute that is used in episodes that involve Krishna or those that have forest settings.[4] I have also heard the *singā*[5] or horn and the bugle being used, but these are still quite uncommon. The dance arena (*āśór*) is marked out with wooden posts. It is hard, dry ground usually near the Shiva temple. Petromax lamps are used to illuminate the arena. The dancers use a minimum of props, other than the elaborate masks that they wear and the gold and silver embroidered costumes. The space around the arena is left empty for the audience to sit. As the evening progresses and the excitement mounts, more and more people enter the arena, to sit where they can get a better view of the dancers. The *māchhās* – string cots hoisted on long poles, form a semi circular gallery behind the seating area on the ground.

Let us now turn to the performance. It usually begins at around eleven o'clock at night and carries on until daybreak. There is a burst of music as the troupe approaches the arena where the dance is to be held. The drummers announce their arrival with frenzied drum beats, the wind instruments wail and the masks are held aloft and shaken till they quiver. The musicians circumambulate the arena, playing their instruments. This is called the *tāla bhāṇgā*. It helps to 'set' the *āśór* (*āśór jaumānó*) – to create the necessary excitement for the dances that will follow. The music frames the dance, dissociating the space and the time of the dance from the other activities that are going on side-by-side in the temple precincts.

As the musicians enter the arena for the *tāla bhāṇgā*, the *ḍhol* players prance backwards and forwards, beating their drums and uttering short, sharp exclamations of *chhāu*. The *dhamśā* and *śainā* players walk around the arena and then either sit or stand on one side and play. Then the singer comes in and welcomes the audience to the performance with a special *jhūmūr* song.

Ṣūnó, ṣūnó śaubāgaun, śaubé kórī nībedaun
Hāmra dīn hīn aubhāgaun hé
Apnādér āmóntron pé, hoyā anónditó móné
Hāmrā ékhāné kórechī āgômaun hé
Ṣūnó, ṣūnó bóndhugaun

Oh listen, all you assembled here, accept our offering
We are poor and unfit
Having received your invitation, with gladdened hearts
We have come here
Oh listen all you friends

After this the singer may immediately begin another *jhūmūr* to introduce the dance that is to follow. However, before I actually give the song and describe the episode that it introduces, I will briefly summarise the story on which it is based. The story, Parashurama's sighting of his *guru*, Lord Shiva (*Parashuramer Guru Darśana*), is popularly used to begin dance performances because it incorporates an invocation (*vandana*) to Lord Ganesha. Ganesha is traditionally worshipped before the beginning of new ventures and all performances begin with an invocation to Ganesha.

The story is as follows: Shiva and Durga retire to their private abode in the Kailash mountain, having instructed their son, Ganesha, to stand guard outside to prevent intruders from disturbing them. Parashurama, a hot tempered ascetic, chooses this moment to visit Kailash and demands a meeting with his *guru*, Lord Shiva. Ganesha, in an excess of zeal, tries to use force to prevent him from entering his parents' abode, but Parashurama defeats him with contemptuous ease. Kartikeya comes to the aid of his younger brother, Ganesha, but he too is unsuccessful in stopping Parashurama. Finally, it is Shiva himself, awakened by the sound of battle, who succeeds in vanquishing him. But in the process Parashurama achieves the purpose of his mission, a sighting (*darśana* or *daurśaun*) of Lord Shiva.

The *jhūmūr* song that is sung at the beginning of this episode is given below:

Āgé té baundónā kórī Gaunés gaujānaun
Tārpauré baundónā kórī Sībéró chaurón
Tārpauré baundónā kórī Kārtīk chūḍānaun
Tārpauré baundónā kórī Pauróṣurāmó débógaun

Tārpauré baundónā kórī jautó debógaun
Nómó, nómó Nārayaun
Ṣīndūró baurónó aungó, mūṣikó bāhón
Śaukól śidhidātā, Hauró Gourīró naundón

First, I invoke Ganesha, the elephant headed
Then I invoke the feet of Shiva
Then I invoke Kartikeya, whose head is adorned with a crown
Then I invoke Parashurama and other gods
Then I invoke all gods in existence
Narayana, I salute you
With vermilion hued body, whose vehicle is the mouse
Who grants all wishes, the son of Hara (Shiva) and Gauri (Durga)

By the time the song has ended Ganesha has taken up position at the entrance, half crouched, one leg extended, shoulders quivering expectantly.

The *ḍhols* begin a steady beat as Ganesha advances, pacing. He crouches, moves his head to display the mask, an elephant head with a halo around it, decorated with tinsel beads and small plastic flowers. This is the *chhauk* or display. It is followed by a few *ḍégs*, that is, a series of jumps that end in the crouched position with the right leg extended. By this time the *ḍhols* have increased their tempo.

As Ganesha slows down to the *ūḍāmālaut* – pacing around the arena with a deep knee - bending walk, the *ḍhols* also slow down to a measured beat. Ganesha does *ulfās* (high leaps), *bāhimnaukā* (the quivering of the shoulders especially associated with the heroic gait) and *éḍi ghórā* (turning on the heel). Each time the dancer completes a particular sequence of steps, the *ḍhols* stop and the *ḍhol* players shout *chhāu.*[6]

At this point in the performance Ganesha, frozen in one pose, is ritually worshipped (*āratī*). This is the real invocation and Ganesha at this moment is set apart from the role that he has in the episode that follows. It appears that this worshipping is a recent interpolation in the dance episode. This is clearly marked by the music for the *ḍhols* and the *śainā* stop playing, giving way to the *kaurneṭ* or clarinet on which a Hindi film tune is played. Also, the dancer who enacts the role of devotee worshipping Ganesha dances in a style modelled on the dance sequences from popular Hindi films with elaborate hip swinging movements not otherwise found in the *chhó* dance.[7] After this the episode continues.

Kartikeya, as befitting the commander-in-chief of the gods' army, enters in a burst of peacock feathers. His dance is even more vigorous than that of Ganesha. He has peacock feathers attached to his mask and costume. This is known as the 'false Kartikeya dance' (*naukól kārtikér nāch*). It is not necessary for the unfolding of the story but only added to the dance episode more to show off the skill of the dancer and the splendour of his costume.

A roll of drums beats (*dhamśā* and *ḍhol*) announce Shiva's entrance. He takes the Nataraja (the Lord of the Dance) pose with a trident in one hand. His dance consists of sudden movements followed by a swing back to immobility.

Shiva instructs Ganesha to stand guard while he retires to his own abode in Mount Kailasa. Nandi and Bhringi (Shiva's demonic followers) are to help him. Nandi and Bhringi are comic characters with grotesque masks. They adopt a splay footed gait, swinging their hips like puppets. They perform a caricature of the heroic gait, yet with an awkwardness that is more characteristic of the animal gait. Shiva, Ganesha and Kartikeya use natural hand gestures, so Shiva points his finger as if in instruction. This provides narrative continuity, but the sudden switch from Shiva's statuesque pose to this pause can seem incongruous to the outsider.

There is another roll of drums in anticipation of Parashurama's entrance. He enters with nonchalance and makes a mocking gesture at Nandi and Bhringi, who try to take up menacing postures. He pushes them back, scornfully. The pace quickens as Ganesha enters the arena. The war beat drummed out by the *dhamśā* drowns the *ḍhols* and the *śainā* as Parashurama defeats first Ganesha and then Kartikeya, who comes to his brother's help, in a series of wild *ulfās* that threaten almost to break through the boundaries of the arena. As the music reaches a crescendo Durga enters with her vehicle the lion and then Shiva. The battle draws to a close and the *śainā* player plays the tune of the devotional song *Raghupati, Raghava, Raja Ram,* to mark the reconciliation. Parashurama has achieved what he came for – Shiva's *darśana.* All the characters shake hands. Then the other gods come in and all the dancers dance the *mél chhó* to celebrate the peace. (The *mél chhó* is a group dance in which all the dancers synchronise their steps.) The end of the dance is fast and heavy, and the air is thick with dust. The words of the songs that are sung and the style of the singing all make the performance a patchwork of different tonalities. As we saw, the dancers enter the arena on a note of challenge – the *tāla bhāṇgā*. But this changes to supplication with the invocatory *jhūmūr*. The dance is offered as a gift to the audience. Therefore the performance always begins with a Ganesha *vandanā* but the episode that has been described here is not particularly complimentary to Ganesha. His first dance that ends with the *āratī* is set apart from the rest of the dance, in which he is shown to be an inexperienced warrior easily overcome by the seasoned Parashurama. And the war scene is mixed with comic elements. Thus even at the height of battle when Shiva and Durga enter the arena to support their sons against Parashurama there is a side play in which Nandi and Bhringi try to pull the lion's tail and fall back in alarm when it pounces on them.

Purists like Bhattacharya have deplored the assimilation of inauthentic elements in the dance – novel gestures like the handshake between Parashurama and Ganesha in the episode described above for example, or pieces of popular film music. However, if we view the dance not as a single homogeneous entity but as a composition of heterogeneous pieces, we see that these novel elements do fit into the overall structure of the dance. Take the example of the handshake, which has become one possible mode of greeting among men. The dance transforms it into a gesture that symbolises the peaceful resolution of the conflict. The fact that this gesture is accompanied by the tune of a devotional song made popular by Mahatma Gandhi, a symbol of nonviolence himself, is singularly apt. Again, take the Hindi film song sung at the time of the worshipping of Ganesha. It seems slightly incongruous coming as it does at that point in the performance, soon after the rhythmic beat of the *ḍhol*. Yet the structure of the dance allows for sudden breaks in the musical rhythm and, thematically at least, the song complements the ideas expressed in the invocatory *jhūmūr*; since the words of the song, "Let the evil eye not fall on my beloved's face" (*têrī pyārī pyārī sūrat kó kisī kī nazar nā lagé*) though originally addressed to the romantic heroine by the hero in the film *Chaudhvin ke Chand* can also be interpreted at a more spiritual level to refer to the relationship between God and his/her devotee. Not only does the performance allow for direct audience participation by shaping itself in terms of the response of the spectators but in a fundamental sense the dance also acknowledges their life world by incorporating musical elements like popular film songs into its structure. Together, both spectators and dancers create the performance. Meaning is generated playfully in the spirit of *līlā* (divine play), which is the goal of all ritual performances in this culture.

'THE PRIMITIVE WAR DANCE': ASHUTOSH BHATTACHARYA'S REPRESENTATION OF THE CHHÓ

In the previous section I tried to enter the field of performance by presenting an ethnographic description of one particular enactment. I will now move to another register and for the rest of the chapter will deal only with the way in which the dance enters written discourse. By describing one particular performance in detail I have tried to highlight a crucial element – the dance presents a series of iconic images that are polysemic in nature. No written discourse can capture the fullness of the images presented. But even this statement is loaded, emerging as it is from a particular disciplinary perspective on culture and community. I am aware that my description assumes that this dance form is culturally distinctive and is therefore embedded in a bounded community whose members all partake of a system of shared symbolic meaning. Thus even accretions like the introduction of Hindi film songs and so on are integrated seamlessly into the dance form making it an organic whole. However, my purpose in this chapter is not to present a critique of anthropological representation but rather to describe the process by which the dance form circulates in a public sphere via the written discourses of folklorists like Ashutosh Bhattacharya.

Ashutosh Bhattacharya and those who come after him have tried to construct a history for the dance. This 'history' is not an objective or a chronological account of the dance but rather one particular mode of creating intelligibility. It has its own imaginative tropes. His writings on Purulia *chhó* are numerous and address many different types of publics, ranging from fellow folklorists, to students of Bangla literature and even to uninformed audiences who might be watching Purulia *chhó* for the first time. (In fact, he is as famous for his role as an impresario who was the first to expose this dance to audiences abroad as he is as a specialist on the folk culture of Bengal.) However in spite of their range, his writings on Purulia *chhó* are remarkably homogeneous and revolve around a few themes, which I will try and summarise.

He calls it a "ritualistic and calendrical" dance performed before, "the village shrine with the purpose to induce the primitive sun god (now Hinduised to Shiva) to produce more rain for agricultural purposes" (Bhattacharya 1975: 10). Bhattacharya's hypothesis is that the *chhó* originated with the Doms. This group, he says once formed the infantry of the local chieftains of this region but were forced to disband and were reduced to their present status when the British pacified this region in the eighteenth century. Then he goes on to say that, "A local tribal chief who ultimately rose to the status of a Raja was a great patron of this dance. In his zeal to spread Hinduism over his people he introduced the Hindu legends from the epics into the theme of the primitive war dance" (1975: 11).

He also develops on the theme of the *chhó* or as he terms it the 'Chhau' being a tribal war dance by analysing the term philologically. 'Chhau' may refer to 'Chhauni' – a military camp. He sees in the dance, the remnants of various other kinds of martial art forms that are no longer found in Purulia. The dances are like "simple morality tales", he says – they articulate the play between good and evil. But more than the dance it is the mask that becomes the focus of his imaginative reconstruction. He includes the *chhó* in a comparative perspective that will encompass all masked dances everywhere in the world. With reference to the *chhó* mask he says,

> The Chhau dance once held the mask to be an object that was inherently holy, but that was when they were made of wood. Now wooden masks are only artefacts which are preserved in shrines.... They are taken out only on special days for ritual dances... when craftsmen carved the masks from wood, they were revered and passed from father to son.... Today the masks are made from papiér maché by a method unknown elsewhere (1975:12).

Ashutosh Bhattacharya's writings on Purulia *chhó* are inflected by his self – proclaimed status as the 'discoverer' of this exotic dance form and, therefore, as the one who must mediate between it and the outside world. The theme of the exotic – the mask as being quintessentially exotic – is addressed to a foreign audience. Bhattacharya's own feelings towards the dance, the masks and the people these belong to, in however, deeply ambivalent. In some of his writings in Bengla he refers to the mask as a disguise that the dancer can use to hide his own dark visage so that he will not appear incongruous when he tries to represent the gods.[8] The mask helps him to take on the image of the sacred. Yet at the same time, for Bhattacharya, the mask is a sign of distortion. If at one level it serves to hide the disjunction between tribal and Hindu cultures at another level it reveals it more clearly. The *chhó* dance, he says, can never aspire to become a classical dance form because it prevents the face from being integrated into the total bodily expression of the dancer. At times Bhattacharya's discourse is overtly racist. In his account of masked dances in Eastern India he compares the *chhó* with the Manipuri dance form. He feels that there is some similarity between the *chhó* and the Manipuri dances as they both contain a mixture of Hindu and tribal elements. He says, however that the Manipuri dance was able to develop into a classical art form because the fair complexioned Manipuris could take on the appearance of the gods in the dance without having to resort to the use of masks. He seems to imply that the physical appearance of the aboriginal people of Purulia is directly related to the form that the dance has taken and to the stage of development that it has been able to reach (Bhattacharya 1965: 762).[9]

However my intention in this section is not so much to expose Bhattacharya's writings as false but to reflect on his orientation to the phenomenon that he seeks to explain. Is his kind of historical reconstruction a mode of explanation? Does it qualify as a mode of history writing? Gadamer (2000) says that the condition of unintelligibility often motivates scholars to take a detour via the historical, at least for those who have inherited the Romantic tradition. What makes sense can be understood at sight and what does not can be understood as survivals or contradictions from the past. Bhattacharya's plunge into historical reconstruction may have been an attempt to come to terms with what was for him an unexpected and even puzzling juxtaposition of two incommensurable cultural formations – 'primitive', 'tribal' culture with 'civilizational' Hinduism. It is in these terms perhaps that one can view his attempts at mediation. Hence, the location of Purulia *chhó* within the Dom community, at present, a low-status caste group within the Hindu-fold, and its later appropriation by tribal kings; or the enigmatic references to wooden masks, which no other authority on the dance form ever mentions.[10]

Needless to say, for the dancers that I knew in Purulia, there was no rupture between the aspects of so-called primitive religion and the high tradition of Hinduism. They viewed the dance as a whole and not as reified in its various aspects. The masks were not seen as sacred per sé. They became one of the attributes of the sacred icons that were embodied in the dance. The word for 'mask' in Purulia is *mūhā* which means face. The masks become the faces of the dancers in the course of the performance. As a dancer told me once, "The masks that you see are dead, they will come alive again when we put them on in the evening to dance".

THE CHHÓ AS A SYMBOL OF TRIBAL CULTURE

Bhattacharya's representations of the dance are meant for an alien audience. It is interesting to observe, however, that when other writers write on the *chhó* dance for an audience that is presumably familiar with this dance form, the same themes are repeated.

I shall take up one such work. Bankim Mahato (1978) as a cultural activist and a proponent of a unified Jharkhandi identity, takes a very different political stance from that of Bhattacharya but still follows his example when he reduces culture to a collection of customs and rites which are treated as the collective property of a particular group and symbolically seal its boundaries. He speaks of a unified cultural area Jharkhand, of which Purulia is a part. The *chhó* dance belongs to this cultural area and is an ancient and magical (*indrajālik*) dance so that the gestures used tend to demonstrate an event or achieve a particular aim which is to bring rain. The author turns to early folklorists like James Frazer and Jane Harrison for support in his speculations about the original purpose of the dance. This he discovers in its form, which he says is mimetic. The linear sequence in which the dancers appear in the performance is supposed to imitate the pre-monsoon clouds (*kālboiśāki*) which chase each other across the sky. The music of the *chhó* dance (by which I assume he means only the drums) simulates the thunder that accompanies the pre-monsoon showers. The mimetic connection between the dance form and the forces of nature is magical because the tribal's will is so strong that he forces nature to obey. He has no need for prayer and supplication. He quotes Frazer for support.

> Magic assumes that in nature one event follows another necessarily and invariably without the intervention of any spirit or personal agency. Thus its fundamental conception is identical with that of modern science, underlying the whole system is a faith, implicit but real and firm, in the order and uniformity of nature.[11]

There is no disagreement between Bhattacharya and Mahato about the outline of the history of the dance, only disagreement regarding the values given to the two cultures – tribal and Hindu.

Bhattacharya was often puzzled by the fact that such primitive people were able to preserve 'classical' Hindu themes in their dance and to portray them correctly. This, for Mahato, is a sign of the degradation of tribal culture, and of its exploitation by outside forces. Both authors give the dance homogeneity in terms of form as well as in terms of participation in the dance. This is far from actual reality. The dance has never been restricted to any one caste or tribe, and it has a structure that can easily absorb outside influences.

Bankim Mahato, as I have said, is a scholar–activist who speaks for the distinctive Jharkhandi identity of Purulia's culture, separate from that of West Bengal. In the early eighties when I was doing my fieldwork in Purulia, the debates and discussion around the *chhó* dance were largely located within Purulia itself. *Chhatrak*, a journal published from Purulia was the only forum in which such debates were published. Twenty' years later, when I began to re-examine some of the issues that I had worked on in my doctoral dissertation, I found that not only was there an explosion in the written literature on issues pertaining to the culture of Purulia but also that writings on the *chhó* dance were appearing from other districts of Bengal and Bihar, like Jhargram, Keonjhar, Kolhan and so on. (This is over and above the three traditional regions where the *chhó* is supposed to be located and which are associated with the three canonical styles that this dance form takes – Purulia in West Bengal, Mayurbhanj in Orissa and Seraikella in Jharkhand.)

In an earlier paper on the *chhó* dance I had said that the discourses on the dance form generated authoritative representations that were later absorbed into the form itself such that by the time I was doing fieldwork in the 1980s it had become what it was represented as – a war dance. I then went on to show how this had led to a diminishing of stylistic variation in Purulia *chhó* such that some of the more difficult dances were no longer performed (Chatterji 1995). After having read some of the new literature on the *chhó* dance I have to reconsider my earlier statement. The homogenisation of the dance form has occurred side-by-side with its proliferation, not merely in Purulia, as I had previously discussed, but also in other regions. Its relocation has led to further transformation in the dance style so that we may have to speak of multiple styles within Purulia *chhó* itself.

Is this proliferation an effect of publicity? The circulation of representations of the *chhó* dance creates new publics who lay claim to this dance form. Added to this, the composite nature of the form – the fact that it can absorb new elements, but also shed them - makes the public domain a suitable site for the articulation of cultural politics. By claiming ownership of the *chhó,* dance communities stake claims to a distinctive identity – one that self–consciously thinks of itself as other to Bengali high-culture.[12] They claim an originary primitiveness that marks their culture out as authentic. However this form of authenticity is never embedded in an interactive community but rather in a territory which becomes the space of an abstract community and a 'composite culture created out of an amalgamation of different types of 'boundary–crossings' between contiguous groups. Thus, Pashupati Mahato (2001) speaks of the *hara–mitan* or the quality of human fraternity that characterises Jharkhandi culture, in fact he uses this Kurmali[13] term as a designation for the composite culture of the region. In a different vein Mahua Roychaudhury (1996) finds traces West Bengal's composite culture in the *chhó* dance. But for her the notion of composite culture refers to the interchange between folk and classical forms of culture over time, specifically with reference to dance rather than to inter-community exchange in the present within the context of a bounded space.

Pashupati Mahato is a cultural activist and a specialist on the culture of Jharkhand as was Bankim Mahato before him. Also like the latter, he presents it as an autonomous cultural region with only a superficial affiliation to the folk culture of West Bengal. However, what sets him apart from the earlier activist writers in Purulia is the position that Ashutosh Bhattacharya occupies in his writings. The latter is his chief interlocutor, the 'other' against whose negative representations, Jharkhandi identity must crystallise. (Bankim Mahato, as we have seen, never referred to Ashutosh Bhattacharya by name.) Let me give an example,

> Bhattacharya... reconstructing the history of the origin of Chhó dance traced it back to Buddha drama. (It) has a very ancient origin, which can also be guessed from comparative study of the origin and development of two other ancient forms of Indian dance – Manipuri of Assam and Kathakali of Kerela ...the system which is followed in Chhau dance today could not have been developed by the aboriginal people who practice this dance. It is indeed a contribution of a higher culture keenly conscious of an aesthetic sense.
>
> (Mahato 1987: 71)

He also refers to Bhattacharya's Bengali text of 1965 that I have also mentioned in an earlier section – the one in which the latter says that the tribal dancers wear masks when depicting characters from the Puranas since their own 'black' faces would not be equal to this depiction. Bhattacharya goes on to say that there is further proof of this hypothesis from the fact that the dancers do not wear masks when depicting events or stories that are purely local. (Needless to say, I found no basis for this assumption. The only time a dancer does not wear a mask is when he is performing pure *nritya* and is not enacting a specific character.) Mahato (1987) quotes extensively from Bhattacharya's writings to show how Bengali folkloristics has a political agenda, that of appropriating the tribal voice. As he says Bhattacharya's texts still form part of the curriculum for the post-graduate course in Bangla literature in Calcutta University. To counter this kind of representation Mahato seeks recourse to another source of authority, to the famous exponents of Purulia *chhó* about whom he has an insider's knowledge as well as to scholars who come from this region. Interestingly, Mahua Roychaudhury (1996) refers to one of the famous exponents of Purulia *chhó*, the late Gambhir Singh Mura, whom Mahato also mentions, as an authoritative source for her own reconstruction. As I have already mentioned, it is diametrically opposite to that of Mahato. She quotes from the interview she had with Gambhir Singh to establish the historical link between a folk form like Purulia *chhó* and a vanished classical dance that was once performed in Bengal. She attributes the disappearance of Bangla classical dance to the effects of colonisation, to the indiscriminate adoption of western culture by the Bengali *bhadralók* and also to the popularity of north Indian musical and dance forms that came to Calcutta in the wake of the Nawab of Avadh, Wajid Ali Shah's being exiled to that city by the British. Both these movements, she says led to the neglect of Bengal's original high culture and to its subsequent demise.

Both Mahato and Roychaudhury share a common concern, which they address from opposite vantage points. They both think of culture in terms of its location in a territorially bounded space, that is, in terms of an ethnic boundary. But this space is a virtual space, waiting to be embodied in practice and in representation. Instead, scholars like Mahato and Roychaudhury have, through their writings, helped create a discursive space that points to the emergence of a new public sphere.

Orsini (2002) says that one of the most significant features of the public sphere is the emergence of a common language of debate. This creates a common horizon, a virtual space that allows public activism a certain freedom from the limits of participation in the face-to-face context. Virtual space is clearly liberating – it allows for critical debate, there is an awareness that one is accountable to a public out there. Yet it is also alienating – the public being addressed is composed of faceless strangers.[14] Thus the need to anchor one's discourses in some form of institutional authority. In the two discourses mentioned above, the source of authority is tradition – embodied in the voice of the exemplary dancer. The difference between the earlier writings – of Ashutosh Bhattacharya, but equally that of Bankim Mahato, and that of the younger scholars, is the explicit use of quotation and citation to establish the legitimacy of their claims. They are more self-consciously polemical, far more aware that the object that they are writing about is being constituted through the circulation of the discourse itself. I see this change in the style of representation as evidence for the crystallisation of a new public sphere, with Purulia as its centre. The expansion of the space in which the discourse circulates does not inevitably lead to its homogenisation, in spite of the fact that there are only a few common themes that circulate. There are instead multiple publics, constituted by the easy transferability of the common theme from one site to another. In the process, the theme itself undergoes multiple transformations. I have already touched upon this when I discussed how communities who claim to perform the *chhó* dance have multiplied over the years. Let me now demonstrate this in more detail, taking one specific theme that recurs in most of the public discourses on Purulia *chhó* – that of ethnic identity.

THE BIRTH OF THE ADIVASI: THE CREATIVE APPROPRIATION OF TRIBAL HISTORY

Recent writings on the public sphere in India tend to focus on the development of literary languages and the emergence of reading/writing publics (see Naregal 2001, Orsini 2002). Instead, I intend to focus on dance performance – the emergence of a public that is responsive to the writings on Purulia *chhó* but is not necessarily literate. The influence of written texts extends beyond the boundary of a literate public, as I will show in this section, when the dancers respond to what is written about the dance through the dance itself.

As I have said Ashutosh Bhattacharya literally created a tradition for the dance, not merely through his writings, though their influence is far reaching, but also through the dance festivals he organised. Schecner describes a dance performance that he saw with Bhattacharya in the village Matha in 1976.

> During the dancing he sits behind a desk, two petromax lanterns making him the best lit figure of the event, and next to him are his university assistants. All night he watches and writes. The next day, one by one the villagers appear before him.... He warned one party not to use story elements not found in the Hindu classics. He chided another for not wearing the standard basic costume of short skirt over leggings decorated in rings of white, red and black. Bhattacharya selected this basic costume from one village and made it general. When I asked him about it he said that the costumes he chose were the most authentic, the least Westernised... (1983: 89).

Other scholars located in Purulia have also tried to reconstitute/recover a tradition for the dance by suggesting themes of historical significance such as the Santhal Rebellion of 1956.[15] A dance episode on this theme was, in fact, choreographed by Nepal Mahato, a student of Gambhir Singh Mura, in 1979. It was performed before a group of folklorists at a conference held in Purulia town. But it has not been accepted at the popular level. Thus, even though new themes are constantly being introduced into the dance tradition and even interludes with Hindi film songs have been accepted, contemporary history is not considered a source, which can provide authentic themes for the dance.

Why do compositions like "The Santhal Rebellion" have no authority for those who are integrated in this dance tradition? Gambhir Singh Mura, the leader of the dance troupe in Chorida, the village where I did my fieldwork, once said to me, "When people ask me, 'From where have you taken the *rauś* (flavour), *tāla* (rhythm), *bhóṇgi* (style), *chāl* (gait) of this dance?' What shall I say in reply?" For him the authentic form of the dance can only be revealed by the *paurānic* and epic texts. This is not to say that history has no place in the consciousness of the dancers. In response to the efforts of folklorists to bring innovations in the themes, the Chorida troupe created a new dance episode that they called, "The Origin of the Adivasis" (*adibaśir utpótti*). However, the history that they constructed was a mythic history based on a narrative found in the *Sharaboli*, a sacred text.

The process by which a narrative location was found for this idea will described in some detail. The choreographer of the Chorida troupe, Anil Shutrodhar was initially thrown into confusion because he could not find any reference to the word 'adivasi' in the *Brahma Vaivarta Purana* that deals with the origin of all *jātis*. He finally consulted an elderly Brahmin who dismissed the problem by saying that the word 'adivasi' had been coined by Mahatma Gandhi and therefore could not have been used in the Puranas that are ancient texts. However, Anil Shutradhar was able to recollect a story from the *Sharaboli* that contained a reference to the Pāśan (stone, rock) *jāti*.[16] He made a connection between the word 'pāśāna', the tribal *jāti* 'Bhumij', to which Gambhir Singh belongs, and the more generic term 'adivasi'. He said that the name 'Bhumij' contained a reference to the aboriginal origin of the *jāti* because it meant 'born from the earth' (*bhuiṇ théké hóeṇchṇe,* i.e. 'bhūiṇ' is the earth). Therefore, 'Bhumij' means 'adivasi'. Rock or stone (*pāśāna*) is their symbol (*pratīka*) because their bones are buried under rocks. The Pāsāna *jāti* mentioned in the *Sharaboli*, can be taken as a reference to the Bhumij *jāti*.

The reference to written texts like the *Sharaboli* and the *Brahma Vaivarta Purana* seem to contradict my earlier statements about the emergence of a non-literate public around the discursive formation that Purulia *chhó* has become. However, it is the fact of being written rather than what is written that is important here. When Anil Shutradhar consulted the *Brahma Vaivarta Purana* it was an act of memory – the text as it exists in the collective memory of the village, as the embodiment of tradition and as a standard against which performance can be measured. Writing, the notion of a book, acts as a distancing device, it constitutes tradition as being set apart - objectifying it and making it self–reflexive. Tradition becomes a constituent part of the public, it exists to be addressed. This, at least, is the way I have tried to make sense of Gambhir Singh's hypothetical questions.

The constitution of the *chhó* dance as an object of public discourse is crucial in the kind of innovation described above. But a question still remains – why is Purulia *chhó* singled out when there are many other dance forms in Purulia that have not become discursive objects? It may, perhaps, have something to do with the composite form of the dance. Different aspects of the form are in a relationship of dissonance, which makes for the easy absorption of new traits. This fact is important in the re-constitution of the tradition. Let me go back to the new dance *pālā* that I just described. The ground for the mythic appropriation of new issues such as ethnicity had already been laid even before the troupe started experimenting with new compositions. The mask makers of Chorida have tried to make profit from the outsider interest shown in the *chhó* dance by making small scale masks of human 'tribal' faces which they sell in Purulia town. This has had some influence on the iconography of the dance masks as well. Rishis, *munīs* and other human characters depicted in the dances are now shown wearing masks with human features such as wrinkled brows or smiling faces with teeth that are supposed to resemble human teeth. I may mention here that gods are usually depicted with closed mouths and *asuras* are depicted with fangs or a single white slab without any demarcation of individual teeth. More significantly for my argument, there is one dance *pālā* for which the Chorida troupe is famous – the episode in the *Mahabharata* when Shiva appears before the hero Arjuna, disguised as a *kirāta* (tribal) to test his prowess before the great war. Shiva as *kirāta* is depicted as a 'tribal' hunter and wears a full–scale version of the curio mask (Chatterji 2003). As this example shows the introduction of the commodity form may sometimes have a positive effect on folk culture, precisely because the power it has to de-contextualise and alienate. In the process it opens up new spaces for innovation. Even though this innovation is often radical it is not disjunct from the tenor of everyday life. The power of popular culture comes from its familiarity, the intimacy associated with day-to-day practices. Forms of folk culture that have the potential of recovering this relationship of intimacy with their publics will flourish. Those that cannot will perish or be reduced to folkloric exotica.

NOTES

1. Unlike the more common designation 'Chhau', my spelling of the word is closer to the way it is pronounced in Purulia.
2. Ritwik Ghatak, the film maker, used the motif of Purulia *chhó* in at least three of his films. He used it symbolically to portray both primeval innocence as well as primitive savagery, in films that had no overt relationship to tribal culture. More recently, Bangla theatre

has also used the *chhó* as a literary device to talk of communal violence. In a Bangla play called 'Riot' by Shashi Thakur, the main protagonist is portrayed as a Muslim *chhó* dancer who is attacked by Hindu fanatics for daring to portray the characters of Hindu gods in the dance (cf. Samaddar 2004). The use of the *chhó* to represent the tension between folk simplicity and violence seems to have become a stable literary device.

I am grateful to Rimli Bhattacharya for bringing the review of this play to my attention and to Poulomi Chatterjee for explaining the use of *chhó* in new dance re-constructions like *Goudiyo Nrittya*.

3. The spelling is phonetic to depict the way the word is pronounced in Bangla.
4. A metonymic relation is established between the flute, the aboriginal hunter and the forest in many narrative genres in Purulia.
5. It is interesting to observe that some scholars think that the *singā* was the original wind instrument used in the Chhó at the time when it was still a 'war dance'. They believe that it was replaced later by the *śainā* when the dance became more stylised and began to use pauranic and epic themes (Chattopadhya and Sinha 1979).
6. Perhaps this is the reason Ashutosh Bhattacharya calls the dance form 'Chhau'. I have never heard the dance being designated in this way in Purulia.
7. The dancer who performs the *āratī* is known as a *densār* (from the English word 'dance') and not *nāchuāḍ*, the term normally reserved for *chhó* dancers.
8. The association between light skin and civilization and dark skin and savagery is an important theme in the colonial history of India (Trautman 1997). I do not think that it has been adequately problematised in Indian scholarship. Colonial modes of addressing race and culture occur as unconscious traces in the writings on folklore and popular culture as we have just seen in the case of Ashutosh Bhattacharya's. One finds traces of this mode of thinking even in more recent works. Thus Sumanta Banerjee (2002) finds evidence of goddess Kali's aboriginal origin in her dark skin.
9. Lokendra Arambam, with whom I had the opportunity to speak during the conference on folklore and the public sphere organised by the IGNCA and the NFSC in Delhi in October 2002, said that in Manipuri dance, the face itself, is treated as a mask.

   Needless to say, the *chhó* is not danced exclusively by 'tribal' people. The dance troupe that I worked with had dancers from all *jātis* in the village.
10. I think that Bhattacharya sometimes conflates accounts of the *chhó* dance with the dances performed during the Gambhira ritual in North Bengal. Like the Shiva *gājón*, when the *chhó* is ritually performed, the Gambhira is a Shaivite ritual. The Gambhira is of

historical significance in Bengali folkloristics. An account of this ritual was first published in a monograph on folk religion in 1916 by Benoy Sarkar. Sarkar finds traces in this ritual of Bengal's early religious history. Thus Buddhism and Jainism, the two great religions that precede Hinduism in Bengal are still supposed to be alive in folk memory (Sarkar 1941, Chatterji 2003).

11. The author does not give proper references for his quotation. I presume that he is referring to Frazer's major work, "The Golden Bough".

    Frazer believed that the evolution of the human mind went through three phases – that of magic which was based on the coercion of natural and supernatural forces, religion which was based on supplicating them and science which reverted to compulsion. He felt that even though magic was based on the mistaken application of two fundamental laws of thought, that is, "the association of ideas by similarity" and "the association of ideas by contiguity in space and time", it still presented a more objective view of the natural world than did religion. He said that it was similar to science in its belief that the mastery of the world was possible. Religion, for Frazer, represented a retrogressive stage in mankind's evolutionary history (Mauss 1972).
12. This is variously defined either as Sanskritic or colonial depending on whether the dance is claimed for the articulation of an originary Jharkhandi or Bengali identity. Purulia, being a border district (between West Bengal and the new state of Jharkhand) is the site of conflicting territorial claims.
13. The link language between different communities in this region.
14. Warner (2002) defines the public sphere as the space created by the circulation of discourse. It is a space of encounter in which different genres of texts and discourses address each other. It is unlike the space of localised face-to-face interaction because its reality lies in the fact of reflexive circulation. The addressable object of the discourse is conjured into existence in this process – "to enable the very discourse that gave it existence" (2002: 61).
15. The Santhal *hūl* or rebellion of 1856 was led by the two brothers, Sidu and Kanhu, who proclaimed that they had divine sanction to guide the destiny of their people.
16. The story that contained this reference is as follows:

    Surabhi, the celestial cow lived in the retreat (*ashrama*) of the ascetic Jamadagni, Parashurama's father, Raja Kartaviryajana, had gone hunting with his entourage and took shelter in Jamadagni's retreat for the night. The celestial cow, Surabhi produced food to feed the King's entourage, golden palaces for them to shelter in and servants to provide for their comfort. In the morning all this disappeared and only the ascetic's hut was left. The king coveted the miraculous cow.

But the ascetic said that he could not give away what had been given to him by the gods. The king was confident that he could take her by force. But she produced soldiers – from her udders (*udor*) emerged the Ujjan, from her eyes (*chokhu pauthe*) the Chauhan and from her hooves, when she stamped them, the Pashan.

2

Between Myth and History : The Making of a Goddess Tradition

Bhadu and Tushu are the two local goddesses whose worship marks some of the significant phases of the agricultural cycle in Purulia. Bhadu is worshipped in the rainy season at the time when paddy seedlings are being transplanted and Tushu, after the harvest crop, in winter.[1] In Chorida, the village where I did my fieldwork, Bhadu is worshipped mainly by middle level Bengali *jātis* (Bhatts and Sutradhars)[2] and Tushu by *jātis* lower down in the caste hierarchy such as Doms and Ghasis as well as 'tribal' *jātis* like the Bhumij. Apart from the caste specific nature of their worship, however, they are remarkably similar in some of their features. Both are virgin goddesses, worshipped exclusively by women and the songs sung during the rituals associated with them are by and large the same. However, Bhadu, unlike Tushu, is also thought to be an aspect of the great goddess Durga by her worshippers.

Bhadu and Tushu rituals occupy an important place in the print culture of Purulia in that they are often used to exemplify Bengal's distinctive location within pan-Indian civilization. In this regard they form a set. As a pair of virgin goddesses they are sometimes opposed to mother goddesses like Durga while at other times the term of opposition is between them. However, even as an oppositional pair their status vis-à-vis each other is that of a privative rather than an equipollent opposition (Barthes 1967).

Tushu as the representative tribal figure is the unmarked term from Bhadu is derived.

Thus the Bhadu *pūjā* (worship) is described as an offshoot of aboriginal festivals that still occur in the border regions of Bengal, in the districts of Bankura, Birbhum, Burdwan and Purulia (Bhattacharya 1965, Kar 1994). Making a comparison between the Bhadu and Tushu *pūjās*, Bhattacharya (1965) says that Tushu is the original harvest festival of this region associated with a specific set of ritual practices and songs. Tushu, according to Bhattacharya, is not really a goddess. She has no iconic form and no origin myths that support her worship. Bhadu, on the other hand, does have an origin myth, but one that describes her as human and she thus has anthropomorphic form. Bhattacharya says that some of the elements (specifically songs) broke loose from their tribal moorings and were appropriated by low status Bengali *jātis*. Thus, for him, Bhadu *pūjā* is not a proper ritual anchored in the agricultural cycle. Rather it is a secular festival, organised by young village women for their pleasure. However, over time, he says, it has come to acquire the trappings of Hindu idolatary (*poutóliktā*) such that Bhadu has been given anthropomorphic form and the status of a goddess.

The Bhadu complex occupies a double position. On the one hand Bhadu is linked by metonymic association to local 'tribal' rituals and on the other to the pan-Indian goddess tradition. The Bhadu complex emerges through the articulation of different systems of representation. In one Bhadu is represented as a sacred icon and in the other as an indexical sign or a historical trace to be deconstructed by scholars who are interested in delineating Bengal's pre-history. In this chapter I shall focus on the myths and songs associated with the Bhadu *pūjā* and their inscription within an emerging print culture that purports to historicise Bhadu. Together, songs, myths and 'historical' accounts of whom or what Bhadu really was, make up a complex system that I shall try to unpack in the following pages.

Why is there such an interest in historicizing Bhadu? Is it because her origin myth presents her as a human woman who is transformed into a goddess after her death? I believe that this endeavour is part of the historical project of Bengali folkloristics that, since the nationalist period, has tried to present folk religion as secular and pragmatic. This representation is used to counter dominant images of India as predominantly spiritual and other-worldly (Sarkar 1941,1985). Scholars like Benoy Kumar Sarkar (1985) think of

Hinduism as offering a grammar, which allows the folk to articulate their worldly concerns through the images of so-called 'Hindu' gods.

THE MOTHER GODDESS TRADITION

The mother goddess traditions in India occupy a unique position within the sociology of religion as they form a bridge between the great and little traditions (Beane 2001). In this sense the Bhadu complex merely replicates the structure of the larger goddess tradition. Thus Humes (1998) shows how a local goddess becomes Vindyavasini, develops a textual, Sanskritic tradition and becomes a pan-Indian figure, without, however, losing the qualities that anchor her within a specific region. Even Indologists and historians of religion who have studied the philosophy of shaktaism tend to place the mother goddess complex at the confluence of two distinct streams of Indian civilization – the Aryan and the non-Aryan (Coburn 1988, McDaniel 2003, Bhattacharyya 1973 and Beane 2001).[3] Thus as Coburn (1988) says that even though it is generally agreed that the origin of the goddess traditions lie in India's non-Aryan, non-Sanskritic pre-history, there has been a continuous interplay between the two streams such that it is difficult to distinguish between the indigenous culture and that of the invading Aryans. Instead, he prefers to use the sociological concept of 'Sanskritisation' – to characterise the process of textualisation that transforms the goddess tradition at a certain point in time. He uses 'Sanskritisation' in its literal sense – the rendering into Sanskrit and describes this as one of the chief methods of re-affirming a tradition in terms of a sacred past. To re-discover an ancient lifeline to an original truth as Coburn puts it.

I too am concerned with the textualisation of a goddess tradition but one that charts a different trajectory – from the sacred to the secular. I explore the process by which 'history', so-called – the realm of the everyday, replaces the realm of the sacred and becomes the source of 'original truth'. What do I mean by this statement? The texts that I seek to analyse in this chapter tend to place everyday life within the domain of history, reason and truth telling. They oppose this realm to myth – the realm of fiction or story-making at best.[4]

In Purulia, however, myth is a mode of truth telling (*kathā*) and is opposed to *kahānī* or story making (Chatterji 1987). Myths interact with daily life. They demarcate the realm in which folk gods and goddesses become directly accessible to their worshippers (Chatterji 1987, Sontheimer 1997). The perspective from which I present my argument could broadly be designated as the phenomenological approach to myth (Piatigorsky 1993, Cantlie 2003). Thus myths form a separate province of reality with their own objective structure of consciousness.[5] They co-exist with the everyday but only as discrete fragments. In the phenomenological approach myths are estranged from the traditional contexts of their occurrence. Rather, they are "symbols" or "enclaves in a province of reality with a completely different meaning structure" (Schutz and Luckman 1973: 127). As Schutz says, mythic themes and particular religious experiences sometimes leave "enclaves" or "gaps" in the everyday world. These are represented through symbols, as the relevance structures of this world are inadequate to articulate them. This gives them an aura or a phenomenological sense of transcendence (Schutz and Luckman 1973).

However, Schutz also says that the experiences or themes of everyday reality leave gaps in the other provinces of reality. He does not elaborate on this provocative statement. It can, however, lead to new and exciting ways of tracking the path between the province of myth and daily life. I suggest that the re-narrativisation of the Bhadu theme, through the search for its historical roots, may be part of a new social imaginary that involves the construction of new social myths (Castoriardis 1987).[6]

The narrative that I take up for analysis is the 'origin' myth associated with the goddess Bhadu whose worship is prevalent in the border districts of West Bengal, viz. Bankura, Birbhum and Purulia, as well as in the adjacent parts of Orissa and Jharkhand (Chakravarti 2001). I juxtapose this myth with a set of songs that form part of the ritual complex associated with her worship. In a sense the myth and these ritual songs provide two different kinds of contexts through which the form of the goddess is configured. That is, simultaneously, as local and universal. All the myths presented below were narrated to me in the course of my fieldwork in Purulia.

WHO IS BHADU?

Bhadu, who is thought to be the beloved daughter of the Maharaja of Kashipur, died unmarried. Her memory is kept alive through this *pūjā*, instituted on her birthday. The enigma of Bhadu's virginity and untimely death has led to many variations in the story that purports to explain it. In this section, I give an account of the range of stories I encountered in Purulia. In these stories Bhadu's divinity and her existence as a flesh and blood woman occur on parallel registers. This co-existence is not thought to be problematic. Bhadu partakes of the nature of the archetypal mother goddess whose entanglement in the day-to-day lives of her devotees is celebrated in all goddess festivals in Bengal.

Let me begin with some stories - origin myths that seek to describe Bhadu's complex identity as both human and divine.[7] One set of stories view Bhadu as an incarnation of the goddess Durga who was born in the house of the Maharaja of Kashipur in answer to his prayers.[8] Being a goddess she could stay with him for only a limited period of time. She died a virgin because no mortal man would have dared to aspire to marry her. Another version draws parallels between the story of Bhadu and that of Mira bai, the Krishna devotee who has achieved semi-divine status in the popular consciousness. Bhadu was devoted to Lord Krishna and she had no eyes for mortal men. The priest at the temple of Krishna, in Kashipur, heard her voice in the temple at night and was convinced that she met her lover there. He informed her father, the king, but when they forced open the doors of the temple they found her dead body in the arms of Lord Krishna.

Bhadu *pūjā* comes just before another festival, Chhata *parab* (*pārvan*), which takes place on the next day. It is supposed to be a royal festival – the raising of the royal umbrella in celebration of a victory in battle. At present, it is performed in most villages in Purulia. The juxtaposition of these two *pūjās* has led to their being combined in one story. Bhadu's marriage was arranged. On the wedding day when the groom arrived, Bhadu saw that her husband had the form of an umbrella (*chhāta*) and killed herself. (The narrator of this variant told me that the rituals performed on Chhata *parab* are the same as those performed when greeting a bridegroom.)

The descendants of the royal house of Kashipur also have their versions of the story. The traditional version states that Bhadreshwari (Bhadu) was the daughter of Maharaja Bikhambar Narayan Singh Deo. She was to be married but her bridegroom died on the way to Kashipur. She remained a virgin and all men viewed her in the form of the Mother, as Devi. She was thought to be a *maha sati* when she died. She was born on Bhadra *saṅkrānti* and died on the same date. This is the date on which the *pūjā* is performed.[9] But the narrator went on to question some aspects of the story. Why should a cucumber be sacrificed (*kāṇkūr bali*) in the course of the ritual, if the *pūjā* was for a mortal and not for a deity? As she explained, sacrifice (*bali dāna*) is only performed during the worship of gods.

The same narrator knew another version of the story, told to her by the family priest, which to her, sounded more plausible. One of the Maharajas (unnamed) had been away from his kingdom for a considerable length of time, fighting the enemy. All the adult males of the family had gone with him. The women of the royal family performed Gauri *pūjā* for their protection. During the *pūjā* they got the news of the Maharaja's victorious return from battle on the day of Bhadra *saṅkrānti*. To commemorate his victory he raised a white umbrella, a symbol of Shyam Raghuvar Deo, and their *kula devatā*. From this the custom of raising the *chhātā* (umbrella) on Bhadra *saṅkrānti* spread, perhaps, she said, Bhadreshwari was born on this date and the two events, Gauri *pūjā* and Bhadu's birthday became conjoined in the course of time. The Gauri *pūjā* was performed by women because all the men were away from home at that time and to this day it remains a women's festival.[10]

The enigma of Bhadu's untimely death is important not only within the oral narrative tradition of Bengal but it has become important in its print culture as well. In the following section I approach Bhadu through another set of stories, this time scholarly exegeses of her iconography, her origin myths and above all her, the songs that accompany her worship. The attention given to her songs in these scholarly accounts indicate a process of humanisation in which Bhadu becomes the exemplary Bengali woman. Thus her songs come to embody the everyday experiences of rural women folk, they speak of their emotions and their subjectivity. In sum, the songs come to represent the archetypal woman's voice.[11]

BHADU'S PUJA

> All our rural festivals (*utsav*) are tied to the golden crop (paddy). Our rural folk have poverty, drought and flood as their daily companions, yet their radiant humanity shines through their festivals (Ghosh 2001: I).[12]

This quotation is from the preface to a book on Bhadu published by the *Folk and Tribal Cultural Centre* sponsored by the Government of West Bengal (Chakravarti 2001). This institute has played a significant role in sustaining and even reviving folk art forms in West Bengal as I have already said. One of their major activities is to document all aesthetic and religious forms that can be thought to represent the voice of Bengal's folk. Bhadu *pūjā*, as an exclusively woman's ritual, has long excited the attention of the Bengali intellegentia and there exists a considerable body of literature on Bhadu. Collections of Bhadu songs in print are a more recent addition to this literature.

Before I discuss the significance of Bhadu songs for Bangla folkloristics in greater detail, a brief account of the ritual is in order. The actual *pūjā* is usually performed by a group of families who share the costs and the work involved in organising the *pūjā*. The festival continues all night and groups of women sit with Bhadu, singing songs to her, eating sweets and performing the ritual. The ritual itself is not very elaborate – it involves an *āratī* for Bhadu, performed by one woman in the group. (Bhadu is worshipped with incense. A lamp filled with clarified butter and incense sticks are circled before her.) Her feet are anointed with oil and turmeric and sometimes with *sindūr*. No *sindūr* is put in the parting of her hair, as Bhadu was unmarried. (My informant made a point of distinguishing this aspect of Bhadu's *pūjā* from the Durga *pūjā* in which the women devotees engage in *sindūr* play (*khélā*) with the goddess.) After the *āratī*, a cucumber is sacrificed before her icon (*mūrti*). Bhadu is worshipped three times in this way, in the course of the night. The first time when her *mūrti* is installed, then at around 11 p.m. and finally at daybreak before the *mūrti* is immersed in the village pond. There is considerable rivalry between the different groups of Bhadu worshippers. Young girls visit each other's Bhadus singing songs in praise of their own Bhadu while disparaging those of their rivals. These form a special genre of song called *liyayī geet* (quarreling songs). It is said that this is the one night in the year when women can roam the streets freely because men are too scared to come out of their houses. Indeed, the year (1981) when I participated in the *pūjā*, the men of the family with which I was staying, sat huddled in one room while the women took over, moving from one house to another. Young boys sometimes set up a rival *pūjā* with Bhada (a masculine variant of Bhadu), so that they too can participate in the *pūjā*. But Bhada is not a god and is not worshipped in the way that Bhadu is.

This is one occasion in which women of the Bengali *jātis* can sing songs in public. The songs are mostly joyful, sung in a group. Bhadu is addressed as a young and beautiful woman, sometimes as a young bride, come to celebrate the *pūjā* with her parents and friends. However, some women compose songs especially for this occasion. Sometimes these songs commemorate an event of great significance such as the celebration of a special festival for the first time in the village or a birth. In 1981, when I was in the village, one woman sang a song of supplication, pleading with Bhadu to give her a son. (She was mother to six daughters.) Since songs play such an important role in Bhadu *pūjā* it is to this that we now turn. Folklorists tend to view these songs as the medium for women's self-expression and thus associate them with the subaltern voice. But before I discuss this in further detail let me set down a representative sample.

BHADU SONGS

In most folkloric accounts of the ritual, the songs are supposed to embody the essence of Bhadu *pūjā*. In fact, as Subrata Chakravarti (2001) says, in his authoritative account of Bhadu *pūjā*, the songs take the place of *mantras* in her worship.[13] In her songs, Bhadu is portrayed in many forms but most often as a young bride who returns to her natal home for the brief period of her festival.[14] Thus,

Āmār Bhādū, āmār Bhādū,
Ké baulé ré kāló ré
Bauddómānér hólūd éné
Gā kórībó āló ré

My Bhadu, O, my Bhadu
Who says that you are black
I will bring turmeric from Bardhman town
And make your body glow

Kéndó nā, kéndó nā Bhādū
Chókér kājól jābé gó
Tómār bābā, aubhāginī
Kājól kóthāé pābé gó

Don't cry, don't cry Bhadu
The *kājal* around your eyes will run
Your father, O blighted one
Where will he get you more *kājal*

Often, the figure of the young bride takes on the visage of Sita going into exile with her husband Rama and her abduction by Ravana. Or more infrequently, Radha, sporting with her companions in Vrindavana. In the two songs that I give below on the theme of Sita's exile and abduction, Ravana is likened to the husband who comes to take the beloved daughter away and is addressed in the same way that the bridegroom is addressed in wedding songs.

Kīśé sóṇdhyā dībó gó kīśé sonḍhyā dībó
Hāmār hāte śónār jāṇtī
Āj kī Rāmér ódibāś
Sónār pālki runu jhunu
Rām chóle jāé bónóbāś
Auśok bóné pāté kūirā
Sitā pāśā khélé chén
Jógīr béśe Rābón éśe
Sitā haurón kóréché
Sitā légché bhāl kóréché
Sitā rākhyó jautóné
Dekbó dekbó sónār noukā
Dibó ré dāhān kóré

With what shall I do the evening *pūjā*,
O with what shall I do the *pūjā*
I have a golden betal nut-cutter in my hand
Is today, the day of Rama's coronation
The golden palanquin tinkles as it goes
Rāma is going into exile
In the Ashok forest, in the hut of leaves
Sita played *pāsā* (cards)
In the guise of an ascetic Ravana came
Abducted Sita
He has taken Sita he has done well
But keep Sita with care
Or I will see your golden boat
I will make it sink

(The last two lines in the song may seem obscure. Sita was taken to Lanka in Ravana's flying chariot not in a boat. I think that some of goddess Durga's imagery has crept into this song. Each year when Durga comes to earth to participate in her festival, she travels on one of four *vāhanas* (vehicles): the swing and horse are inauspicious, while the boat and elephant are auspicious. That year Durga was to come on a boat. I remember that the senior woman of the family with whom I celebrated Bhadu *pūjā* told me that Bhadu was another form of Hara Gauri, that is, Durga.) In the next song Yama, the lord of death comes in the place of the bridegroom to take Bhadu back to his kingdom.

Āylyó ré ghūr ghūryā pókā
Dókkhin dīkér bātāśé
Āylyó ré śónār pālkī
Bhādu dhón ké légīté

The earthworm has come
With the wind from the south
The golden palanquin has come
To take our darling Bhadu away

The *ghūr ghūryā pókā* is similar to an earthworm and is supposed to be Yama's *vāhana*. As I have mentioned in a previous section, in some versions of Bhadu's story she kills herself because her bridegroom is unsuitable. The disjunction that most women face, between the familiar natal home and the harsh, often frightening, world of one's husband and parents-in-law is expressed in these songs. The goddess is portrayed as the archetypal daughter through whom women express their feelings about conjugality. It is perhaps slightly ironic that it is only at a time of joyous festivity, when women are free of the restraining presence of their men-folk that they are able to articulate such sentiments.

These songs have a complex thematic and can be read on several different registers. At one level they can be used as evidence to demonstrate that Bhadu's origin myth has no organic link with her festival, and indeed this is the most common interpretation of these songs as far as the scholarly literature is concerned. Bhadu's songs are seen as the archetypal voice of women, expressing their existential situation. However, a closer reading of the lyrics reveal the presence of several motifs, such as death and conjugal separation, that is present in the origin myth. These motifs are woven into the *Ramayana* story. Thus, Sita and Bhadu become interchangeable in some senses because their destinies are the same. Ravana, Yama and Rama too become equivalent, as each one in turn is the figure through which the woman's disjunction is expressed.

The final song that I present in this section is very different from the ones that I have discussed thus far. This song is taken from Ashutosh Bhattacharya's collection.

Āṇkh bāḍité dhāk bājīché éi āśīché Bhādū dhón
Daekh dékhī ré Brójér bālā kautó dūré Brindābón
Brindābónér bóndhū tūmī brindābóné bāś kauró
Kébā tómār mātā pītā kār bā tūmī āśā kauró
Kār ghauré gīyé chhīlé mā ké kóréché śebā gó
Hāté māér rauktó chaundón gaulé jaubār mālā gó
Kāśipūré dekhe élām ṣonār thhālé bāgh bóśé
E bāgh tó mānūsh khāenā rūp daekhāté éśécé
(Bhattacharya 1965: 77)

The drums beating in the bamboo grove hereld
the coming of my treasure Bhadu
Look, look Vraja maiden, how far is Vrindavana
You are a friend of Vrindavana, you live there
Who are your parents, whom do you look to for support
Whose house did you go to, who took care of you
Ma's hands are stained with red sandlewood paste,
She wears a garland of red hibiscus flowers
I went to Kashipur and saw a tiger sitting on a golden plate
This lion doesn't eat people, he has come to show himself

In the discussion that follows Bhattacharya expresses his puzzlement about the lion motif in the song. Why should Bhadu be likened to a non-man-eating lion he asks? His answer is that like the children's rhymes found in Bengal's countryside, Bhadu songs do not always have meaning. I will take up the issue of the architectonics of the songs in the next section when I discuss the relationship between voice and primordial consciousness. However, Bhattacharya's refusal to acknowledge what seems to be an emphatic and repeated reference to the goddess Durga is surprising. Foe example, the line in the song that describes her garland of red hibiscus flowers and the reference to Durga's *vāhana* (vehicle), the lion. Bhadu is never adorned with red flowers, only white ones. Red flowers are usually restricted to the great goddesses like Durga and Kali. (Also, Bhadu is never shown with a *vāhana* – even though she is sometimes shown sitting on a lotus flower like the goddess Lakshmi.) The opening line of the song that refers to Radha and then the references to Durga seem to suggest that Bhadu is thought of as part of the goddess complex. "All goddesses are one," I was told in Purulia. "Who is Bhadu? Hara Gauri in one of her many aspects."[15]

The inscription of Bhadu into the Bangla print culture has initiated a process of desacrilisation. Her biography, the fact of her being human is stressed and the mythic aspects of her story as well as the rituals associated with her worship, such as the cucumber sacrifice, are passed over in silence. To his credit Ashutosh Bhattacharya (1965) does not fall pray to this mode of rationalisation. He views Bhadu *pūjā* as a tribal agricultural festival that is transformed by Hindu iconicity due to the colonising efforts of the Rajas of Kashipur. But the strict separation that he makes between the tribal and the Hindu elements has led to the disaggregation of the ritual complex in the scholarly literature. Bhadu songs are foregrounded in the analysis and the rituals that anchor them within a specific context are ignored. The emphasis on the songs especially on the lyrics have also helped to crystallise a particular disciplinary perspective which assumes that folklore is necessarily concerned with the search for the authentic voice of the people. The manner in which this is done and the process by which the feminine voice becomes the privileged site for the recovery of this authenticity is the subject of the next section.

BHADU: THE VOICE OF SUBALTERN FEMININITY

The study of women's rituals first became important in Bangla folklore in the early decades of the twentieth century with the nationalist studies of Indian civilization (Chatterji 2003). Women's rituals (*vratas*) become an important source for examining Bengal's unique location within pan-Indian civilization. Thus Abanindranath Tagore (1919) privileges domestic *vratas* performed exclusively by women as the pure (*khāñṭi*) rituals that have managed to escape the reach of the shastric tradition. As evidence of this he cites the songs and rhymes that take the place of *mantras* in these rituals. Thus rhymes such as:

Rāi ūṭhhéchén rāi uṭhhéchén Bauḍó gauṇgār ghāṭé
Kār hāthé ré tél gāmchhā dāo gó rāier hāthe
Rāi utḥhéchén rāi uthhéchén méjó gaungār ghāté
Kār hāthe ré śāñkhā śindūr[16] *dāó gó rāiér hāthé*
(quoted in Roy 1972: 118)

Rai (the sun) has risen, Rai has risen, on the main Ganga *ghāt*
Who has the oil and the towel? Give them in Rai's hands
Rai has risen, Rai has risen, on the middle Ganga *ghāt*
Who has the conch shell bangles and the red virmillion?
Give them in Rai's hands
(and so on)

According to Tagore, this rhyme shows traces of animism. It refers to a time when the world of nature was not separated from the human world. Thus, Rai (the sun) is likened to a married woman taking her ritual bath, anointing her body with oil and adorning herself with sindoor. Tagore's book, *Banglar Vrata* has become a classic in Bangla folklore studies. Later folklorists have used this work to re-construct the pre-Aryan culture of Bengal (see Roy 1972 for instance). Border regions like Purulia acquire special significance in this re-construction as they are thought to be living museums preserving the sources of Bengal's history and culture. I shall elaborate on this theme in another chapter. Here, I will briefly discuss one of the major theories about the 'aryanisation' of Bengal as it relates to the theme of women's *vratas*.

According to this theory, the first Aryans to enter Bengal were not Vedic Aryans but rather Vratyas who did not perform the fire sacrifice like the Vedic Aryans and spoke in a different dialect. Their religion was probably closer to the animistic cults that were already prevalent in the Austric-Dravidian culture of Bengal and, in time, these amalgamated and evolved into a syncretic culture and worldview that could pose a challenge to Vedic Hinduism (Sinha 1997). In fact, as Sinha (1997) goes on to say, it is not accidental that the two great religions that opposed Vedic Hinduism, viz. Budhism and Jainism, originated in Eastern India. The Aryans of the North, designated the Kuru-Panchala region mentioned in the *Mahabharata*, were only able to pacify this region by incorporating their gods and rituals into the Hindu fold (see also Roy 1972). However, some of the rituals and beliefs that were perhaps closest or most intimately related to the everyday lives of the people of this region were removed from the public domain so that they would not be sullied by the new Brahminical religion. The domestic sphere, the sphere of women, became the protective space in which they could flourish. The word 'vrata' is traced to 'vratya' to bolster this theory (Roy 1972).

In my discussion of the folkloric perspective on Bengal's cultural history, thus far, I have tried to show how the category of the 'feminine' crystallises as a figure around which particular discourses on identity cohere (see also Chatterji 2003). The feminine domain is the other within, a kind of residual space that was overlooked by the colonising force of Brahminical Hinduism. How does this space, then, become transformed into the site of subaltern resistance? Also, why does Bhadu become the figure of exemplary womanhood? To address this set of questions I must first explore the manner in which Bhadu straddles the realms of both the human and the divine.

Subrata Chakravarti begins his book on Bhadu with a rhetorical question – "What kind of *pūjā* caters exclusively to women, has no priests, no *mantras*, no customs or prohibitions? All you have are songs, baskets full of songs" (2001: 2). He says that it is more like an *utsav* (secular festival) rather than a *pūjā*. Bhadu's *mūrti* is not a sacred icon, instead it is an image of a pretty young girl, a married daughter come to visit her parents. The *mūrti* has no ritual or coded meaning. 'The elders', by whom he means authoritative informants, say that the *mūrti* is for decoration (*śājāno*), for show, that is to lend colour (*rauṇg*) to the festival. (To demonstrate this, Chakravarti says that Bhadu's *mūrti* has no fixed attributes or symbols that can be used to identify her like other goddesses.) He says that the festival (*utsav*) is a way of setting aside a period of time when women can come together freely, away from the structures of patriarchy that constrain their everyday lives.[17] Bhadu, herself, in her biography provides the first tentative steps to what, Chakravarti feels, can develop into a path of female emancipation. But this still does not address the specificity of her birth as a royal princess, and daughter of the house of Kashipur. Why should a Kshatriya woman become the symbol for oppressed womanhood? He offers a tentative hypothesis. Perhaps, because she was popular with the king's low caste subjects; or because she rebelled against the life that was being planned for her; or because she was planning to elope with a low caste man, she was murdered by her own kin.[18] In death Bhadu posed an even greater threat to royal authority than she had in life. The only way in which the king could avert a full-scale rebellion was by incorporating Bhadu into the ritual calander. Yet unlike other rituals, Bhadu's festival carries traces of the same quality that characterised her life – it is irreverent and emancipatory.

In this text, then, Bhadu is an ideological construction, a successful piece of propaganda to discipline and pacify a potentially rebellious population. The institution of her worship can be seen as an attempt to incorporate and legitimise the source of rebellion by royal authority. However, Bhadu does retain her exemplary status, if not as a goddess, than as a figure that represents womankind and by extension all those who are subjugated. Not all scholars are as easily able to dismiss Bhadu *pūjā* as an act of propaganda. I have already mentioned Ashutosh Bhattacharya's theory on the Bhadu *pūjā*. The timing of the *pūjā* – during paddy transplantation, Bhadu's association with goddess imagery, especially the symbols associated with agricultural prosperity such as paddy sheaves that she is sometimes shown carrying in her hands, have led some scholars to think of this *pūjā* as an agricultural ritual, for the propitiation of the newly growing paddy crop. Thus, even though Bhadu's association with the subaltern voice is of recent origin, her association with subaltern practice has a longer history. According to more recent variants of the agriculture theme, this ritual may have been introduced by the *rājās* of Kashipur to motivate their subjects to cultivate a particular kind of paddy crop (*bhādūi dhān*) that is harvested after the monsoons (Chakravarti 2001).

In the various accounts mentioned in this section we see the Bhadu complex being associated with a set of motifs – the woman's voice, subaltern classes, tribal, agricultural festival, royal authority and the archaic past. The relationship between the motifs themselves and with the Bhadu complex in turn, is variable – sometimes a logical conjunction, at other times a contingent association. I wish to examine one strand in this complex association in greater detail that is, the connection between Bhadu and the woman's voice. As scholars like Chatterjee (1993) and Sarkar (2001) have shown the nationalist discourse in Bengal posited a domestic, feminine space that was insulated from the modernising influence of the colonial state. This internal space came to be represented as the space of popular culture and the ground for national resurgence. Bengali folkloristics has not only appropriated this argument but is also able to claim that it represents the authentic feminine voice. Thus women's rituals and songs become the concrete embodiments of the domestic space, which is the source of cultural authenticity.

As I will show in the next chapter, folklore's contribution to the discourse on Bengali womanhood is marked by a certain ambivalence. Early writings on women performers tended to stigmatise their songs as lewd and obscene (Banerjee 1989, Chakraborty 1966). It is only the songs that are tied to the performance of women's rituals that are free of this stigma. Yet even though the domestic sphere is the site on which these rituals occur, they are not contained by it. Bhadu's worship allows women to appropriate public space even if only for a limited period. Her songs subvert domestic relationships, portraying marriage as a kind of death. Also, the archetectonics of the song makes it a suitable vehicle for the expression of public criticism. Consider the following song:

Bāgmunḍi ṭā bóṛó auṇdhókār
Tāṇghāi dībó bījlīr tār
Bāgmunḍi ṭā bóró auṇdhókār
Ākāl kórlé kéné bhaugobān
Pānér dokān chūné bhaumókāl

This Bagmundi[19] is very dark
I will hang up electricity wire
This Bagmundi is very dark
Why did you make famine, O God
The *pān* shops are dazzling white with *chūn*

(The last line of this song will need clarification. This song, from my own collection, was composed in 1983, when Purulia was suffering from severe drought. It satirises the state of affairs when people are supposed to be suffering great scarcity due to the drought, but are still able to buy so much *pān* (betal leaves), which is a luxary, that the *pān* shop walls are white with *chūn* (lime paste) marks. *Chūn* is spread on the betal leaf and after preparing the *pān*, the shopkeeper wipes his *chūn* stained fingers on the wall leaving a white mark. There are so many fresh *chūn* stains on the walls of his shop that they look white.[20])

As this example shows, in women's songs, disparate events are strung together in a paratactic chain.[21] This gives them a loose structure that allows for the incorporation of lines from other songs making them a truly collective creation. This looseness also means that these songs are ideal vehicles for political and social criticism as cryptic comments on contemporary events get included in them.

The discussion so far has made no reference to Tushu, the other virgin goddess also worshipped exclusively by women. Even though she is called a virgin goddess, there were no stories associated with her life in Chorida.[22] However, her songs are important in the political mythology of this region. They became the vehicle for a political movement in Purulia in the 1950s. Purulia was, at that time, a part of the Manbhum district of Bihar and was only joined with Bengal in 1956. The public singing of Tushu songs on the theme of protest were banned in Bihar, which led to the movement of separation from Bihar being named the 'Tushu Satyagraha' (Sinha 1974).

The appropriation of folklore forms for political purposes is a common occurrence in India (Ashley 1993, Singh 2007). It is a consequence of the nationalist discourse that views the 'folk' as the repository of an authentic identity (Coomaraswamy 1956, Dutt 1990). This discourse can be used strategically to 'naturalise' a political position.

CONCLUSION

In this chapter, I have juxtaposed two kinds of 'mythic' narratives – viz. Bhadu as goddess and Bhadu as exemplary woman who represents the voice of the people. Most folklorists would view the latter as an attempt to deconstruct the 'myth' to reveal its true meaning. However, they are also speaking from the vantage point of a nationalist ideology that has appropriated the voice of the 'folk'. I have tried to delineate the way in which this has been done. In conclusion let me say that the structure of myth often lends itself to this process of re-inscription. Audrey Cantlie (2003), speaking specifically from within the world of Hindu myths says that myth is a kind of 'hierophany' which actualises its events, by presenting them as part of present reality, across time, thus, bypassing any notion of historical succession. Thus myths can travel across different spaces as discrete and objective fragments. Political myth making may not present a hierophany but it does involve a fixation and an enlargement of individuals and events in history (Bannerji 1998).[23] However there is an important distinction between the origin myths that I have presented here and the accounts of Bhadu's life presented by the folklorists not so much at the level of plot but rather in the relation between the myth and its narrator.

Piatigorsky makes a distinction between myths as objective phenomena and stories with a mythic theme. In the first case, "the narrator bears witness to an already existing reality...". In the second case, the narrator is conscious that the events being narrated as myth belong to a particular genre. Thus, the *what* and the *how* of the telling are distinguished (1993: 81-82). The folklorists mentioned in this chapter are conscious of Bhadu's story as a 'folk myth', as being part of 'folk consciousness'. They are speaking from the vantage point of genre. For those who worship Bhadu, she is part of their phenomenal world. But is it also possibly to say that the folkloric exercise of revealing Bhadu's human face is also a way of incorporating her into the world that these scholars occupy? Can we think of these two positions on the same page as it were – as two different ways of occupying the world?

Recent developments in folklore scholarship have tried to re-frame the discipline so that it will be able to study myths as beliefs practices and as specific ways of knowing that empirical analysis may not be able to understand. The exercise of de-construction may itself be based on an implicit assumption – that myths are fiction. This assumption tells us more about the world of the analyst than about the world of the worshipper (Motz 1998).

However, at some level the mythmakers of Purulia and the folklorists discussed here also share in a symbolic imagination. Whether seen as origin myth or scholarly account, there is a direct identification between Bhadu's untimely death and the system of explanation. Is it still possible then, to think of these as separate activities, disjunct types of myths, or are they both part of the same mythic universe? Given the reach of the popular print media, it may well be that the folkloric texts may soon function as meta-narratives incorporating the traditional myths within them.

In the first chapter on Purulia Chhó and the constitution of a new public sphere in Bengal, I was able to establish a link between popular representations of the dance in the print culture and the changing aesthetics of the form. I am unable to do this here. I did see advertisements for a play based on the humanised Bhadu story in Calcutta when I visited the city briefly in 2003 but was unable to actually see it. Also I am not sure whether this has had any influence on the ritual or on the mythic consciousness of the actual worshippers. In the case of the *chhó* dance it was the self-conscious aestheticisation of the form itself, a process initiated by the royal patrons of the dance that helped to secularise the dance form. That is, to allow new political and historical themes to enter the dance form. It is interesting that women's songs that have traditionally been open to the incorporation of political and historical events have not acquired the same significance as a cultural symbol in the political discourse of this region. (The Tushu *satyāgraha* no longer has significance in the political discourse.) Is it because, women's songs are not thought to be self-consciously aesthetic forms, that they have not acquired the status of a cultural symbol in the same way as Purulia *chhó*?[24] In the next chapter, I address this question by examining another musical form, the genre of *jhūmūr* song that also acquired autonomy as an aesthetic form long before the penetration of print culture in Purulia.

NOTES

1. Bhadu is worshipped on Bhadra *saṅkrānti*, the second last day of the month of Bhadra (mid August to mid September). Tushu is worshipped on Makar *saṅkrānti*, the second last day of the month of Magh (mid January to mid February)(see Chatterji 1987).
2. Bhatts and Shutradhars are referred to as the *Baṅgālī jātis* (Bengali castes) in the village, Chorida, because they are said to have migrated to Purulia from the neighbouring district of Bardhman. It is interesting to note that in this case Purulia is not considered to be part of Bengal. In other contexts (e.g. folkloric writing on Bengali culture) Bardhman itself is thought to be part of the border region. The fact that "Bengaliness" is a constructed category is clear from the fact that another *jāti*, the Telis (oil pressers), are also said to have originally come from Bardhman district but are not included in the category of *Baṅgālī jāti*. They are, socially and ritually, of a status lower than the Bhatts and the Shutradhars.
3. The mediating position occupied by the mother goddess tradition allowed nationalist scholars to claim a distinctive place for the culture of Bengal within the civilizational mainstream (Chatterji 2003). Shaktaism is an important religious tradition in Bengal.
4. One must remember that most of these texts are government publications and their authors have sympathy with the ideology of

the Left. However, the characterisation of folk belief as secular has a genealogy that precedes the coming to power of the Left coalition in West Bengal.

5. Phenomenologists characterise our world of experience in terms of "multiple realities". Everyday life forms the "paramount reality" in which we are "wide-awake". However, there are other "finite provinces of reality" that co-exist with the "wide-awake world" to which we escape. Each of these spheres is characterised by a specific tension of consciousness and form of sociality. The movement from paramount reality to one of the finite provinces is experienced as "a leap" (Schutz & Luckman 1973).
6. When I say this I am conscious of the fact that myths are not produced by individuals (Piatigorsky 1993). However, they do undergo major transformations in their re-production and re-enactment (Levi Strauss 1970).
7. All these stories were narrated to me in the course of my fieldwork in Purulia.
8. Kashipur is the capital of Panchakot, one of the erstwhile kingdoms whose territory is included within the district of Purulia.
9. As I have already said the month of Bhadra is from mid-August to mid-September. Saṇkrānti is the penultimate day of a month.
10. There is another variant on the theme of Bhadu *pūjā*, given to me by another member of the Kashipur royal family. Princess Bhadu was left in charge of the kingdom while her father was away, fighting the enemy. This occurred in the month of Bhadra. In Kashipur, the women of the royal family were performing Durga (Gauri) *pūjā* on the day before Bhadra *saṅkrānti*, when they got the news, which turned out to be false, that the king had died in battle. Bhadu, unable to bare the thought of submitting to the enemy, killed herself. Her father got the news of her death on Bhadra *saṅkrānti*, when he returned home, victorious, carrying the symbol of the deity, Shyam Raghuvar, the white umbrella. In spite of his personal loss, the king still had to display the umbrella for all his subjects to view. (The narrator did not explicitly state the connection between the *pūjā* and the raising of the auspicious umbrella, but it seems evident from the story.)
11. The concentration on the songs also points to the crystallisation of folklore within the broader rubric of Bangla literature.
12. All translations from Bangla are mine.
13. On the basis of an analysis of these songs, he characterizes this event as a secular festival (*utsav*) rather than a *pūjā*.
14. Unless specified all songs are part of my collection. I collected these songs while doing fieldwork in Purulia in 1981- 83.

15. Universal and local elements co-exist in the mother goddess complex (Marriot 1955). This is not merely a feature of contemporary folk societies as these folklorists seem to suggest but may have always been the case. Speaking in the context of another deity – Shiva, Sontheimer (1997) says that Rudra, who is sometimes thought to precede the Shiva of Sanskrit texts, may have always been a folk god who lived on in cults like that of Khandoba in Maharashtra.
16. Conch shell bangles and virmillion powder are the symbols of marriage worn by women in Bengal.
17. I find the persistent blindness with what seems to me to be an obvious association with the Durga *pūjā* intriguing. In Bengal, Durga is thought to visit her natal home at the time of her *pūjā*. She is likened to a beloved daughter and her *mūrti* is often the source of artistic innovation such that her traditional iconography is sometimes set aside. Thus, in 2003, I had the privilege of seeing a Durga *mūrti* with lamps of peace in the ten hands instead of the traditional weaponry. As a Bengali from Calcutta, Chakravarti must be familiar with what is considered by many to be the most important and certainly the most public of *pūjās* for Bengalis.
18. One of my informants who is herself a daughter of the house of Kashipur spoke to me of the distress that she as well as other members of her family suffered when they heard of such representations of Bhadu.
19. This is the village in which I lived during the course of my fieldwork.
20. Most dwellings in Bagmundi, when I lived there, were made of mud, plastered over with cow dung paste.
    The unstated reference point of this song is the Great Bengal famine of 1943, contrasted with which the modern notion of scarcity seems somewhat of a mockery (cf. Chatterji 1987).
21. Tanika Sarkar (1999) quoting Carolyn Steedman defines the paratactic chain as a particular syntactic device which is used to describe great contradictions in the nature of events since it can string together a series of contradictions on a chain, linking them up with unsynthesizing 'buts' and so on without trying to make connections between them. Sarkar says that Bengali women writers of the nineteenth century often used this device to critique their lives.
22. I have heard elsewhere, that she was a Hindu *zamindār's* daughter who committed suicide because she did not want to marry the Nawab who was her father's sovereign (see also McDaniel 2003, Sinha 1974).
23. Piatigorsky quotes this fragment by I. Beshtau: "Mythology is given to us in the disconnected fragments of our thought. Their re-connection would mean history" (1993:1).
24. Chakravarti (2001), acknowledge the relationship between extraordinary event and the process of aestheticisation. He says that it requires a trauma of great magnitude to turn ordinary women

into goddesses. Thus, without the trauma of Draupadi's public disrobing in the Kuru court (*vastra haran*) and Krishna's intervention to protect her modesty, the *Mahabharata* may never have been composed. Similarly, it was the scandal caused by Bhadu's love for a low caste man that gave rise to the musical compositions in her name.

3

Jhumur and the Aesthetics of Folk Poetry

In the first chapter on the *chhó* dance, I tried to show how its representation in the bourgeois print culture has led to its circulation within new kinds of publics. This, however, has not led to the disruption of its relationship with its traditional audience. In fact, its entry into the public domain has increased its popularity with village audiences in Purulia at the expense of other dance forms, which seem to be in danger of extinction.[1] In an earlier chapter I have tried to explain this seeming contradiction by relating it to the aesthetics of the dance form. I said that its polyphonic structure, (the dissonant relationship between the music, the dance and the plot) made it receptive to novelty. New musical elements, dance styles and story lines could be easily incorporated into the dance without distorting its essential form. I also mentioned that it was perhaps, royal patronage that had created the conditions in which it could develop into an autonomous and self–consciously aesthetic form (Chatterji 1995).

In this chapter, I will focus on a musical form – the genre of *jhūmūr* songs to explore this question further. Perhaps even more than the *chhó* dance, the *jhūmūr* has the capacity to acquire new contexts of performance. Unlike other song genres that are associated with work and ritual cycles, the *jhūmūr* can be sung at any time (Chatterji 1987). It can be rendered in a variety of different ways and for the intelligentsia of Purulia, it is both a form of high art (that is, it bares traces of *rāga sangeet* and compositions are individually authored) as well as a 'folk' song which is transmitted orally and collectively authorised (B. Chattopadhyay 2001, N. Chattopadhyay 1999). In the chapter on the *chhó* dance I have shown how it crystallises into a tribal war dance and becomes a symbol for tribal identity by excluding certain aspects that are discordant with the image of tribal culture as represented in the public domain – one element being the *jhūmūr* song. In this chapter I use this song form to problematise the very notion of 'folk' and 'tribal' culture as they are articulated in Bengali folkloristics.

Unlike representations of Purulia *chhó* that occur only within a discourse of folkloristics dealing with the culture of Purulia, references to the *jhūmūr* are found in a variety of discourses, scattered on different sites. The two main sites that I take up for discussion are 1) texts that deal with the emergence of popular urban culture in Bengal and 2) Bengali folkloristics. Apart from a somewhat tenuous link via the rubric of 'folk culture', there is no attempt to connect the two sorts of representations of the *jhūmūr*. In the sections that follow, I juxtapose selections from the two types of literature to show how certain features of this composite form are chosen to create a representation that will stand for a certain kind of sociality. This juxtaposition also allows me to focus on the discursive contexts in which the representations occur. Thus different features of the *jhūmūr* may be highlighted or silenced depending on the particular type of discourse in which the representation is embedded. In doing so I do not intend to present a more complete picture of this musical form, rather, I use this as a stylistic device to offer a critique of such concepts such as 'tribal' and 'folk culture' that are part of the larger perspective delineated in this volume.

THE JHUMUR AND URBAN FOLK CULTURE

Sumanta Banerjee (1989) and Sudhir Chakraborty (1966) both refer to the *jhūmūr* form in their discussion on the history of Calcutta's urban folk music as it developed in the nineteenth century. It is significant that the *jhūmūr* is not thought to be an independent musical form in their writings. Instead it is mentioned in connection with the poetical song contests of the *kobiwālās*[2] or the *khemṭā nāch.*[3]

Let me quote Banerjee in his account of the *jhūmūr*. "[It is] variously interpreted as a tribal song and dance performance, or a part of a Radha-Krishna *kīrtana* narrative" (1989: 113). He goes on to quote from the account of a "contemporary observer of a typical street scene in nineteenth century Calcutta".

> They [the *jhūmūrwālis*[4]] were *chhóṭólók* [from the uneducated lower orders], dark-skinned wenches who stank when they passed by. They used to wear anklets around their feet when they sang. In those days during wedding ceremonies, *jhūmūrwālis* used to dance on peacock-shaped papiér maché boats set up on bullock-carts. As they danced, a man from behind used to beat a drum, or strike a bell-metal plate... their language was extremely coarse, but some among them had talents as poets....' He then proceeds to give us a sample of a *jhūmūr* song about Kali:
>
> *Māgī mīnśeyké chīt kórey phélé dīyé būké dīyeche pā;*
> *Ār chókhṭā jūlūr jūlūr, mūkhey nēikó rā.*

(The hussy has thrown the bloke flat on his back, with her foot on his chest. Wordless she stands, glaring in anger.)

(Banerjee 1989: 113)

Banerjee's examples of *jhūmūr* songs are taken from Chakraborty's (1966) seminal work on the history of modern Bangla music. For Chakraborty, musical forms like the *jhūmūr* represent the dark-age of Bengali music.[5] *Jhūmūrs*, along with other forms of popular song and dance become dissociated form their folk-rural roots, according to Chakraborty. They are part of the social upheaval that marks the development of Calcutta as an emerging metropolis. Signs of this upheaval are to be found in the coarse and bawdy lyrics of these songs that have become uprooted from their religious and spiritual environment. However, he does admit that they express popular sentiment and speak of the day-to-day lives of the urban folk.

It is precisely this point that Banerjee (1989) takes up for elaboration. He uses the popular performative traditions emerging in nineteenth century Calcutta to critique the 'Bengal Renaissance'. He feels that the nineteenth century indigenous elite was indifferent to and even actively censored these popular forms of aesthetic expression, thus reducing them to silence. However, in spite of Banerjee's valorisation of these satirical and often bawdy expressions of popular sentiment, there is very little discussion of the musical forms themselves. Like Chakraborty, he merely uses these forms as a counterpoint to the more conservative representations of elite Bengali culture. Interestingly, in both their accounts, the *jhūmūr* is associated with the feminine voice, with a particular kind of dance – the *khemṭā* and with an emphasis on the erotic sentiment (see note 3). I mention this specifically because a very different picture emerges from the folkloric accounts where the *jhūmūr* is largely thought to be a male preserve, with some significant exceptions.[6]

A very different representation of the *jhūmūr* appears in the writings of Gurusaday Dutt. Interestingly, unlike scholars who write about the *jhūmūr* in the context of Purulia, he mentions the *jhūmūr* only with reference to folk dance as part of his larger project on the rejuvenation of the Bengali spirit through her folk culture. I quote:

"The expression of *jhūmūr* is a generic term applied to dances or songs which do not fall under any specific class but are of a miscellaneous character, particularly with erotic association.... The name Jhūmūr may have originated from brass ankle bells making a 'jhūm jhūm' sound on the dancers' feet" (Dutt 1954: 43). Dutt goes on to describe this as a vigorous and acrobatic dance form when performed solo or in duets. He also describes the *jhūmūr* dance performed by Kora women (a caste of labourers, "diggers of earth and makers of roads") that symbolises a close tribal solidarity (Dutt 1954: 45).

Dutt's description of the *jhūmūr* dance must be viewed in the light of his discussion on the folk dances of Bengal and the significance that they were supposed to have for the renewal of Indian society.[7] He felt that the discipline and spirit of cooperation that had once characterised the races of Bengal could still be found in the dances of folk groups of the lower social orders. These had to be raised to the status of a national heritage, for it was around these folk forms that the racial solidarity of the Bengali people had to cohere (Chatterji 2003). Let me elaborate this point.

In *The Folk Dances of Bengal*, Dutt makes a distinction between the court and temple dances of the ancient period with the folk dances of Bengal. He says that Bengal had no imperial court after the eleventh century and, therefore, no imperial culture to lay down a style of dancing.[8] Nor was there a system of establishing temples under royal patronage so that the institution of *devadasis* or temple dancers was alien to Bengal. Thus, "Bengal became congenial soil for the growth of folk dances", a common feature of which "is their vigour and sturdiness and the complete absence of any sensual suggestion either in idea or movement" (1954: 13). He also distinguishes these folk dances from dances like the *khemṭā* and the *nautch*, which, he says were imported into Bengal in comparatively recent times from northern Indian cities, have never been acclimatised in Bengal, and have never become a form of popular diversion (1954: 13-14). As far as Dutt is concerned, the popular urban culture of Calcutta has no place in the constitution of folk culture, and the *khemṭā* dance has no connection with the *jhūmūr*.

Scattered references to the *khemṭā nāch* in association with the *jhūmūr* in works as diverse as those of Banerjee (1989) and Dutt (1954) are significant. This association is used to link not just popular urban culture but even pan-Indian high culture with so-called border regions like Purulia. However, in this section I only want to draw attention to the fact that, as a cultural form, the *jhūmūr* is amorphous. Unlike the women's songs discussed in a previous chapter, it does not appear in the discourse of identity politics.[9] This has something to do with its musical form as I will show. It does become significant, however, in the discussion on the tribal culture of the border regions of West Bengal and its unique position vis-à-vis Bengali culture per se.

JHUMUR AND THE TRIBAL CULTURE OF WEST BENGAL

Ashutosh Bhattacharya's work occupies a significant place in discussions of the tribal culture of Bengal. Not only was he a prodigious documenter and prolific writer but he also had an important role in training the present generation of folklorists in Bengal. His perspective on folk and tribal culture still dominates the field of Bengali folkloristics in spite of the radical 'tribal' voices that are trying to speak out against him.[10] In the different chapters in this volume I have discussed Bhattacharya's accounts of the *chhó* dance and women's songs from the perspective of identity politics. Tribal and subaltern culture is presented as a counterpoint to mainstream Bengali culture – both elite and popular. The two are juxtaposed, even though no intrinsic connection is posited between them.

It is only in his discussion of *jhūmūr* songs that Bhattacharya tries to elaborate on this relationship. For Bhattacharya, the *jhūmūr* song occupies a distinctive place vis-à-vis other song types in the culture of this border region. Its distinctiveness arises from the fact that even though it is a rural folk song (*póllī geeti*) and thus portrays the 'soul' of Bengal's rural folk, it cannot be thought to be associated with any specific form of work or morphological category. This is because the *jhūmūr* is not tied to any caste or tribal group and is non-sectarian. Bhattacharya goes on to say that even though the *jhūmūr* is not a religious song like the *padāvali kīrtana* that is associated with Chaitanya *bhakti*, the Radha-Krishna theme is a popular subject of the genre. This is so because unlike Shiva and Uma or Kali, the other important deities in Bengal who are also portrayed in song, the portrayal of the divine love between Radha and Krishna is not restricted to Hindus. I shall have more to say on this later, but it is certainly true that in Bengal, the divine love between Radha and Krishna forms the subject of a variety of poetic and musical compositions in genres that range from the *fakiri gān* that is sung largely by Muslims, to *baul gān* and even predominantly tribal forms like the *jhūmūr*.

The *jhūmūr* then, is thought to be a collective representation that symbolises the spiritual identity of a whole region. It has evolved within a particular historical context that fostered Bengali–tribal cultural syncraticism. Unlike other parts of India, Bhattacharya says, the tribal groups that inhabit the border regions of West Bengal, voluntarily adopted cultural elements from Bengal and created a vibrant, multilingual culture that remains open to the outside world. The *jhūmūr*, more than any other aesthetic form is supposed to be a product of this cultural hybridity. Thus, the region as a whole, that is, the tribal belt that extends from Chhota Nagpur into Bengal and from Madhya Pradesh up to the border of Gujarat can be called the *jhūmūr* region. It is, according to Bhattacharya, a melting pot, a region in which cultures that represent the different periods of Indian history have come together and intermingled. One still finds Austric speaking populations, the first inhabitants of this region, living cheek-by-jowl with Dravidian speakers who came much later and those who speak Indo-European languages like the Bangla spoken by the Bhumij and the Kurmi-Mahatos of Purulia (Bhattacharya 1965: 134-135). Like the region that it has come to represent, the *jhūmūr* too, is sung in many different languages – Santhali, Kurukh, Bangla, to name a few. However, Bhattacharya's writings do not have a political agenda. He does not try to make a case for the absorption of tribal culture into the mainstream of Bengali culture (Bose 1975, Xaxa 2003). Instead, using the *jhūmūr* form as an example, he carves out a separate genealogy for tribal music and by association, for tribal culture. Thus, if the *padāvali kīrtana* form is the first autonomous song form in Bengal that still has a living presence, then the *Jharkhandi kīrtana*, one of the sub-types of the *padāvali kīrtana* that is now extinct, must have been the *jhūmūr*, he claims. Let me explain the significance of this statement.

Scholars from Purulia say that if the *Jarkhandi kīrtana* is a form of *jhūmūr* then the latter must have an ancestry that pre-dates the *padāvali kīrtana*. As evidence they cite the *Sri Krishna Kīrtana*, the first narrative *kāvya* depicting the Radha–Krishna story. This text is thought to be composed before the fifteenth century, that is, before the *padāvali kīrtana* took concrete shape.[11] However, if the *jhūmūr* form is already associated with the Radha–Krishna theme before the fifteenth century, then it becomes extremely difficult to locate it within the tribal culture of Purulia and by extension, Jharkhand. (The first contact with Bengal Vaishnavism in Jharkhand was made in the fifteenth century when Chaitanya Mahaprabhu passed through 'Jharikhand' on his way to Mathura from Nilachala, Orissa. [Sinha n.d.]) Bhattacharya (1965) circumvents this problem by saying that while the prevalence of the Radha-Krishna theme in *jhūmūr* songs is certainly due to Bengali influence, this tradition did not come to Jharkhand via Hindu shastric texts like the *Bhagavat Purāṇa*. To demonstrate this he gives examples of Santhali and other tribal *jhūmūrs* that portray the erotic emotion. Thus,

Chhetarach natarāch ānkumonroon koyalang
Tumār mamāré chaḍi maumóré tulāng
Hākū maumolāng tulā hāting kuyalāng

(Bhattacharya 1965:135)

(Lover and beloved herd cattle in the forest. They are uncle and niece. The niece says: "Lets go fishing, from the upper pond and the lower pond. We will throw medicine into the pond and divide the catch between us".)

Or the Oraon *jhūmūr* that S.C. Roy has translated into English:

Give him water, mother
Give him water
The flirting boy
Dances the *jhūmūr* all the night
And thirsty he comes
(quoted in Bhattacharya 1965: 135)

It is *jhūmūrs* such as this one that most readily adapt to the Bengali influence. The divine couple, Radha and Krishna take the place of the anonymous lovers portrayed in the tribal songs without any radical transformation in musical form or poetic vocabulary. Bhattacharya uses this as evidence for the hypothesis that the Bengali Hindu influence on the culture of this region did not manifest itself as a form of colonisation. Rather, it took the form of a voluntary and selective adoption of themes that were already familiar to the inhabitants of this region. It enabled the *jhūmūr* to acquire a richer emotional vocabulary. He characterises this as a form of 'bilingualism'. The rest of the discussion describes the various different sub-types within the *jhūmūr* genre. Of these, several are just listed as *jhūmūrs* associated with aspects of the work cycle or with rituals. Three sub-types are selected for more detailed discussion as they are used to make a case for tribal bilingualism. It is also significant that they are not embedded in a ritual context.

Dānḍshalyā jhūmūr is associated with a kind of men's dance and still retains the original form of *adivasi sangeet*, that is, its lyrics portray events in everyday life and do not refer to gods and goddesses. The *chhó* dance *jhūmūr* is always composed in Bangla and is prevalent only in the Bangla speaking areas of this belt, like Purulia. The Bengali/ Hindu influence on the *chhó* dance through the *jhūmūr* is, according to Bhattacharya, probably due to dominant presence of Kurmi-Mahatos in this region. I shall discuss the universe of discourse within which such representations of tribal culture are embedded in later sections. For the moment I merely wish to draw attention to the fact that there is no mention of the *chhó* dance *jhūmūr* in Bhattacharya's discussion of the *chhó* dance as I have said in the first chapter. It is as if the representation of tribal culture when constructed through the prism of the dance must necessarily be monolingual, excluding non-tribal elements from its essential form. The fact that the *jhūmūr* is used to construct a bilingual model that contradicts the first representation is significant. In this context I may also mention that unlike tribal groups like the Bhumij and Kurmi-Mahato, Santhals have kept their own language as the primary medium of communication within their own community and to the best of my knowledge do not consider the *jhūmūr* to be one of their special musical or poetic forms (Sinha 1997).[12] Bhattacharya does mention the *khemṭā* and the *nāchnī nāch jhūmūr*, but in terms that are even more enigmatic than his statements about the *chhó* dance *jhūmūr*. He says that one can sense the trace of the *kobiwālā's* speech in these *jhūmūrs* and that perhaps they emerged to fulfil a "lack" in rural folk society. They embody a particular kind of sentiment that is not found in other musical genres. I will elaborate on this later on in this chapter, but before I conclude this section let me say a few words on Bhattacharya's reference to the Santhals in the discussion on the *jhūmūr*.

He traces an evolutionary course from the tribal *jhūmūr* in Santhali language to the Bangla *jhūmūr* via the Radha–Krishna theme. Shanti Sinha (1997) while referring specifically to Bhattacharya's text, says that the examples of Santhali *jhūmūr* that are given there are not Santhali but rather *dānḍshalyā jhūmūrs* that are more commonly sung by Kurmi-Mahatos. He states categorically that Santhalis do not sing *jhūmūrs*. Let us pause for a moment to reflect on the two terms that seem to occur always in opposition to each other, not just in Bhattacharya's writings but in that of other scholars as well. The Santhals have come to represent the archetypal tribal group in Bengal. They are thought to have an autonomous cultural identity that is also distinct from that of the Bengali Hindu. In contrast, the tribal identity of the Kurmi-Mahato is ambivalent. In fact they are not even included in the list of scheduled tribes in Bengal, as a consequence of their having claimed Kshatriya status in 1931, at the time of the census operation, the last one in which caste was used as a rubric of classification. However, Mahato scholars have been at the forefront of the Jharkhand movement and there has been a movement to reclaim an official tribal identity in more recent times (cf. Mahato 2001). Unlike groups like the Bhumij and the Mahatos, the Santhals are not a dominant numerical or cultural presence in all parts of Purulia. Why do they acquire such significance in these writings then? This may have something to do with the way in which tribal and caste – Hindu interaction is presented in writings of Bangla sociology, even though there is no explicit reference to such work. In *Hindu Samajer Garan* (1949), the influential Bengali sociologist N. K. Bose[13] suggests a model for the understanding of tribe-caste interaction in the border regions of Bengal that has since become known as the "Hindu method of tribal absorption" (Xaxa 2003). He says that overtime many tribal groups were absorbed into Hindu caste society at the very lowest levels. This may be one of the reasons why there is very little difference between the customs of tribal and lower caste groups in these regions. However, the Kurmi-Mahato's who acquired the status of kshatriyas, as well as the Bhumij who became kings and managed to establish a court culture in many parts of Purulia, cannot fit into this model. (The Bhumij are particularly interesting in this regard as they are recognised as a scheduled tribe. Yet they also claim kinship with kings like the rajas of Bagmundi who think of themselves as Rajputs and therefore kshatriyas, as I have shown in chapter one.)

Clearly, Bhattacharya must have thought that the Santhals were more suitable for his model of bilingualism, as they speak both Santhali and Bangla and sustain their distinctive identity while still being able to interact with other groups in this region. But is tribal culture to be thought of as a separate entity within the larger field of folk culture? As I have shown in an earlier work, all Bangla folkloristics is characterised by a certain ambivalence towards tribal culture (Chatterji 2003). Gurusaday Dutt, to mention just one example, valorises the syncretic and celebratory aspects of folk culture. But he only incorporates the so-called secular strands of folk dance in the Bratachari movement so that it would be acceptable to all communities. Dances that involved elements of "magic or superstition" are left out (1954: 8). Similarly, Bhattacharya valorises folk syncretism but is wary of including tribal culture in his model of folk culture. Even though this is not explicitly stated here, there is an assumption that while there is continuity between folk and mainstream Bengali culture, since they represent the aspects of the Great and Little traditions, this is not the case with respect to tribal culture, which is markedly different (Redfield 1955). By focusing on the Santhals, instead of on some other tribal group who might actually be better suited to exemplify his model, he seems to suggest that the tribe is the 'other' against which Bengali cultural identity is to be configured.[14] The Santhals become the symbol of cultural alterity, not just to mainstream, middle class Bengali culture, but to popular or folk culture in other parts of Bengal, as well. (I am thinking of the reference to the *nāchnī nāch jhūmūr* that Bhattacharya says has more in common with *kóbīwālā* songs than the Santhali songs from which the *jhūmūr* originates.)

Quinn, in an important work on the political symbolism of the 'swastika' says that the symbol "functions as a 'structuring absence' whose lack of interpretable meaning is cognitively recognised as a boundary between one set of meanings and another..." (1994:10). It functions as a "recognisable limit" configuring a particular kind of discourse, including those aspects that can constitute it's meaning and excluding that which is not proper to that particular interpretation. In Ashutosh Bhattacharya's account the Santhals seem to function as a symbol that articulates this "recognisable limit" dividing folk society from tribal society. In his representation of the *chhó* dance he selects features of the dance that can qualify it to stand for the archetypal tribal, war dance. As I have shown, the masks, the music of the drums and the dance style are depicted as quintessentially tribal features that set it apart from other folk dances. Even though the stories enacted through the dance are from the Hindu scriptures, these are thought to be a later accretion and do not effect the essential form of the dance.

Bhattacharya makes a distinction between folk and primitive societies. Primitive societies are self-sufficient, traditional and exclusionary; folk societies are open, capable of accepting novelty and are fundamentally non-traditional (Bhattacharya 1962). They are capable of constituting relations with their other and are not threatened by it. Are the tribals of this border region part of primitive or folk society? It is not always clear in Bhattacharya's writings. His accounts of tribal society are filtered through the cultural forms that he focuses on. When he writes about the *chhó* dance, it is in the context of an ideal type representation of a primitive society. But this is not the case with the *jhūmūr* as we have seen. It seems to represent the dynamic features of folk society, without however, being part of mainstream Bengali culture. The Santhals seem best suited to fulfil the role of representative of this ideal.

IS THE JHUMUR A FOLK SONG?

I address this question through a somewhat controversial example – the *nāchnī nāch jhūmūr*. Bhattacharya refers to it in connection with the discussion of the erotic sentiment, one of the dominant moods of *jhūmūr* song, but its connection with the Radha-Krishna theme, the fact that it is thought to be the enactment of the *rās līlā* is not mentioned. I find this puzzling given the significance of the Radha-Krishna theme in Bhattacharya's construction of folk society as being fundamentally heterodox and pluralistic. Thus, this theme, Bhattacharya says, becomes the point of contact between different religious communities – Hindus, Muslims and tribals, precisely because it is used to portray the sentiment of *viraha*, the despair of separation, embodied in Radha's lament when she is separated from her beloved Krishna. *Viraha* or despair (*nirāśā*), according to Bhattacharya, is a living presence in folk sensibility. It combines with the erotic emotion to give a distinctive quality of sensuousness to folk society. Other forms of divine love, like the conjugal love embodied in the relationships between Shiva and Parvati or Rama and Sita, or the maternal love expressed by Kali towards her devotees, Bhattacharya says, emphasize union and can thus never reach out to the soul of the folk in quite the same way. However, when Bhattacharya mentions the *nāchnī nāch jhūmūr*, he only says that it fulfils the same need as the *kóbiwālā jhūmūrs* once did in urban society.

To make sense of this statement we must go back to Sudhir Chakraborty's discussion of the *jhūmūrwālīs* songs. He says that when they sang of the divine lovers they privileged the themes of deceit and dissimulation (*chhalanā*) and stigma (*kalaṇka*). For Sumanta Banerjee (1989) this becomes a mark of the secularisation of urban folk culture. It develops a sense of identity in contrast to elite culture by satirising it. Satire, that uses a particular combination of the lewd and the sensuous, becomes the distinctive signature of popular urban aesthetics. Its unique way of addressing the uncertainty that characterises everyday life in the newly emerging metropolis, Calcutta. It is not as if the satiric mode is not present in folk aesthetics. Women's songs like the Bhadu and Tushu songs that I have discussed in the previous chapter, use the satirical mood to distinguish ritual time from the rhythms of everyday life. But this mood is never mentioned in Bhattacharya's account of women's songs (Bhattacharya 1965). It is as if the lewd and the sensuous must be kept strictly apart. (It would be interesting to explore this point further by connecting it to Dutt's (1954) effort to incorporate a sanitised version of folk culture into his project of nation building, but unfortunately I cannot take it up here.) Is the *nāchnī nāch jhūmūr* another example of the limit that we discussed in the last section – one that problematises the very notion of folk culture? Before we can address this question we need to turn our attention to the *jhūmūr* form itself, its particular architectonics that allows such variation in the way that it can be rendered.

Even though it is formally classified as a 'folk' form (Bhattacharya 1965), the genre of *jhūmūr* song is unlike any other type of folk song found in this region. Not only does it allow for a wide range of musical and thematic compositions but it also bears traces of classical (*mārga*) music. Under the patronage of the local *rājās* it was influenced by the *Vishnupur ghāranā*, the only classical *gharānā* of music in Bengal, and adopted the *rāgā* system (Bhattacharya 1986). Thus the *jhūmūr* includes a variety of musical styles, from the short rhymed couplets usually associated with folk songs in Purulia to elaborate compositions with colophones (*bhônitā*) giving the name of the song composer. Since most folk forms have a collective signature, the use of the personal voice and authorial signature itself gives the *jhūmūr* a distinctive position. It also makes it eminently suitable as a form of *bhakti sangeet*, the personal tone lending itself to the voice of the lover singing of her longing for her absent lord. Even though *vaishnava* motifs are found in most genres of song here, the *jhūmūr* is unique to the extent that its musical structure actually embodies the emotional mood of Chaitanya *bhakti*. Hardy (1983) calls this emotion *viraha bhakti* and says that it expresses a relationship of devotion to a personal deity (Krishna) in the mode of separation. The devotee desires to merge his/her identity with the deity but the fulfilment of desire is indefinitely deferred so that the emotion of separation itself becomes the form of religious experience. Thus, even though the song is addressed to the absent deity, the absence allows the singer to dwell on the emotions of the devotee and since the devotee's voice is his own, on his own emotions as well.[15]

Furthermore, the musical form of the *jhūmūr* itself is designed to enhance the emotion of *viraha*. The distinctive feature of the *jhūmūr* form is its tone (*sur*), the fact that it begins on a high note and then descends gradually to a low note. It does not follow the complete beat cycle (*tāla*) but lingers on the gaps (*phāṅk*) in between to enhance the notes and thus create an impassioned mood. The voice of desire embodied in the *jhūmūr*, the devotees' voice is always a feminine one, since the singer/devotee submerges his/her identity in that of Radha, the archetypal devotee, yet paradoxically the *jhūmūr* is a male preserve. Unfortunately, a detailed examination of the relationship between gender, genre and voice is beyond the scope of this chapter (cf. Chatterji 2002). As I have already said, the musical form of the *jhūmūr* requires a vocal range not normally associated with folk songs in Purulia. Women's songs, for instance, tend to have a monotonous tone with little variation in pitch perhaps suited to the fact that they are rendered in a collective voice. The men with whom I interacted in the course of doing fieldwork said that women are incapable of producing the voice required to sing the *jhūmūr*, which is why it is a masculine genre. While the women did not overtly disagree with this statement, they did say that women's voices are not supposed to be heard by men unless they are raised in unison. The meaning of a song emerges from a combination of musical form, tonality and the lyrics. As Barthes (1990) says, signification arises from the friction between words and tonality. The *jhūmūr* uses this friction to achieve musical significance. Its' lyrics adopt the feminine voice yet its tone and musical form are thought to be masculine. (It will be obvious that *nāchnīs* are an exception to this rule. *Nāchnīs* as public women occupy a liminal position, with regard to the classification of musical genre as well as to society at large as we shall see.)

We seem to have come a long way away from Bhattacharya's formulation of the *jhūmūr* as the archetypal musical form of this region. He is only one among the many scholars of the *jhūmūr* form that consider it to be an incarnation of the ancient *sur* (musical tune) of Bengal. Thus Naranarayan Chattopadhya (1999) says that all the musical forms, all the song types present in Purulia and by extension in tribal Bengal partake of the aesthetic sensibility that is embodied in the *jhūmūr*, that is the sensibility of folk society. The original source of the *jhūmūr* is the primeval folk cry – '*hāñkā jhūmūr*', that still has the quality of improvisation because it arises spontaneously within the group. The examples that he gives are of Tushu songs, that are songs sung by groups of women during the Tushu festival in December-January, while they walk in procession, carrying the Tushu symbol from house-to-house. Thus:

Óṛā kórchīsh kī bākār būkūr
līlāyé dībó pūlīśér kūkūr

(Chattopadhya 1999: 43)

Why are you barking like dogs
(the reference is to a rival group of Tushu singers)
We will set the police dog on you

Or, the example from my own collection:

Dautto bābū, Dautto bābū
Piphā dīlé pīphā nībó nā

Datta babu, O Datta babu
Even if you give us papaya fruit we will not accept it.

Tushu and even Bhadu songs often emerge as spontaneous compositions when rival groups of singers meet on the road, or when particular objects catch a singer's attention and she composes a song that is immediately picked up by the group. The second Tushu song presented above is of this kind. Datta babu, my landlord in the village, had a papaya tree in his compound that many people coveted. He was however very selective in the choice of persons to whom he gave the fruit. A group of Tushu singers who would otherwise have had no interaction with Datta babu, spontaneously composed this song when they were passing by his house. Clearly *hāñkā jhūmūr* is not a concrete song form for Chattopadhya. Rather, it seems to indicate a special musical quality that characterises group singing. He calls this quality, "the call" or "announcement". The next stage in the *jhūmūr's* development is called the *gāhā jhūmūr* or "sung *jhūmūr*" phase. It is not as if *hāñkā jhūmūrs* are not sung. Collective songs that are still sung in work contexts, like the *bhāduriā jhūmūr* songs that are sung while women transplant paddy in the rainy season, still carry features that marked the *hāñkā jhūmūr*. However, as Chattopadhya says, at a certain stage in the *jhūmūr's* development, the primeval folk cry is given an autonomous musical form. This is the form of the *gāhā jhūmūr*. Sub-types of the *jhūmūr* genre that are concrete examples of the *gāhā jhūmūr* phase and which still show traces of the *hāñkā jhūmūr* phase are the *dāñḍ śaliyā jhūmūrs* among others. These songs also take the form of rhymed couplets like the examples of Tushu song given above but they have a more complex musical structure as the text of the song is divided on the basis of the main lyric sung by the main singer and the refrain that is sung in chorus. *Dāñḍ shaliya jhūmūrs* also take the form of musical conversations in which different singers take on the role of dominant voice, so that one singer may start the song but will allow another to complete the line that is being sung. *Dāñḍ shaliyā jhūmūrs* are sung in several different ritual contexts but also on non-sacred occasions. They are songs of passage, sung by groups of men as they walk from one village to another to witness a *chhó* dance performance, for instance or by the men who accompany their womenfolk to the forest to cut the sacred *karam* branch for the *karam pūjā*.[16]

This is the text of a popular *dāñḍ shaliyā jhūmūr* that I heard many times while I was doing fieldwork in Purulia:

Haithé āiló, khāiṭhé boiṣló, kīchhū nā bólīló
ghūmāi gaehéló
Ó mórī mórī, hāi ré hāi, ghūmāi gaehéló
Amār chailyyā jāmāi gó, ghūmai gaehéló
Ó daume ghūmailó

He came here walking, sat down, he said nothing
He fell asleep
Alas, he fell asleep
My young son-in-law fell asleep
He fell fast asleep

According to Chattopadhya (1999), the refrain, "he fell asleep" that is repeated with variations, indicates the work context in which the *dāñḍ shalyā jhūmūr* must have evolved. The refrain sets the pace for the work group. It embodies the rhythm of collective work. In this sense it comes closest to the spirit of *hāñkā jhūmūr*, even though as he says it came to acquire an autonomous status because of its association with the *karam pūjā*. However, the fact that there is a distinct genre of women's song called *jāwā geet* that is sung by women during particular phases of the *karam* ritual, is not acknowledged. In spite of stray references to women's songs like *ṭūshū* or to ritual chants that form part of 'tribal rituals' like *karam pūjā*, Chattopadhya privileges the *dāñḍ shalyā jhūmūr* form as being closest to the spirit of the *hāñkā jhūmūr*. Perhaps, the women's songs that he mentions are too closely associated to their traditional performative contexts to serve as appropriate symbols for a disembodied and abstract ideal of folk community. The *jhūmūr*, given the fact that it is the only musical genre that has acquired autonomy and thus independence from ritual context, is ideally suited for this role.

The last phase in the *jhūmūr's* development is the *bāndhā jhūmūr* according to Chattopadhya, that is *jhūmūrs* that can be thought of as distinctive compositions with the signatures of individual composers, rather than as collective creations. Jhumurs of the *gāhā jhūmūr* and the *bāndhā jhūmūr* phase co-exist in this largely oral culture, Chattopadhya says, and it is often difficult to place particular *jhūmūr* songs in one or the other category. This is because songs circulate from voice-to-voice and individual singers are free to interpolate new passages in songs composed by someone else. Thus in spite of the individual signature *bāndhā jhūmūrs* are also the product of collective creation (see also Bhattacharya 1965). *Bāndhā jhūmūrs* still have direct musical links with *gāhā jhūmūrs* and famous *jhūmūr* composers took ordinary *gāhā jhūmūrs* and transformed them into a highly cultivated musical form – the *nāchnī nāch* or the *darbāri jhūmūr*. The example that Chattopadhya selects for discussion is the *bhāduria jhūmūr* a sub-type of the *jhūmūr* that is sung by lower caste and tribal women when they work in the fields in the rainy season or *Bhādro māsh*. The *bhāduriā jhūmūr* that I give below is taken from my own collection. As the colophon in the last couplet indicates, it was composed by a famous *rasika,*[17] Narottam Singh who belonged to an aristocratic family that lived in Toreng village near the Bagmundi region. He was a frequent visitor to the Bagmundi court. The person who sang this song for me belonged to the Dom caste of musicians. This is a caste of landless labourers, but they are also considered to be the keepers of the great musical heritage of the Bagmundi region.

Ājkér saupónér kauthā
Kī boilbó śoi, ó Nolitā
Bóñdhū āśē pālóṇkhé bóśiló
Nīmāh āgūn jālé dīló
Jautóné dhórīyā móré
Bauśailó nījó kólé
Kī kauthā bólīté nā bolīló
Śéśó kālé móné kórī
Paurāné dhórīte nārī
Nauróttomér dhékté dīn gaeló
Nīmāh āgūn jālé dīló

It is the story of tonight's dream
What shall I say, friend Lalita

My lover came, sat on the bed
The dying embers, he fanned again
Carefully, he took hold of me
Sat me on his lap
What words was he to speak, but did not
I remember the last time
I cannot hold it in my heart
Narottam's days pass by in witness
The dying embers, he fanned again

Chattopadhya (1999) says that the *chanchal* (restless) nature of the *bhāduriā jhūmūr* form can be easily adapted to the *druta laya* (fast tempo) of the *nāchnī khemṭā* dance and becomes a favourite form in the *nāchnī shalyā jhūmūrs*. The *nāchnī shalyā jhūmūr* will be discussed in detail in the next section. However, it is worth mentioning here that, for Chattopadhya, this form represents the culmination of a musical tradition. Tribal sensuality is finally transformed into a self-reflexive aesthetic sentiment. As he says, the *nāchnī shalyā jhūmūr* is *pālā bauddhó*, it is bound to narrative form. The form emplots the erotic sentiment in such a way that the object of poetic inspiration as well as the voice of the poet are both present in the composition, without one necessarily dominating the other. In another context Robert Goodwin (1998) has called this kind of aesthetic form a "spectacle poem". The *rasika's* erotic sensibility allows him to enter the poetic universe as a witness to a divine spectacle rather than as an author of a scene. At first sight there seems to be very little connection between the *hāñkā jhūmūr*, "the folk cry" and the individualised style of the *bāndhā jhūmūr*. Chattopadhya makes no overt connection between them, other than by referring to the aspect of collective creation that is intrinsic to the definition of oral transmission. Thus anyone who can sing the song becomes its author. However, I think the form of the narrative, the fact that it presents the poet as a witness rather than an author gives it a collective signature.

NACHNI SHALYA JHŪMŪR AND THE EMERGENCE OF A COURT CULTURE IN PURULIA

The *nāchnī shalyā jhūmūr* complicates our understanding of folk music and of folk culture as has been represented in this work. On the one hand it bridges the gap between the mundane sensuousness that is supposed to be a feature of tribal life and a cultivated erotic sentiment that is part of an Indian theory of aesthetics.[18] It is both a form of folk music as well as a highly cultivated musical form. On the other hand, its association with a courtesan culture and with the emergence of a feudal aristocracy in tribal central India, makes it suspect to those who wish to draw a line between an exploitative and decadent caste-based society and an egalitarian and innocent tribal society. It is only recently that scholars like Nitish Chakravarti (2001) have located the *nāchnī nāch* firmly within the tradition of folk dance[19] in Bengal, while at the same time acknowledging its indebtedness to the classical north Indian dance tradition developed by the *bāijīs* (dancing girls) that flourished in nineteenth century Bengal.

Nāchnis have an anomalous relationship to the 'tribe', whether viewed as a social formation or as a specific cultural complex. Their art emerged within a feudal system and they thus share in the popular representation of the courtesan as '*patitā nārī*' or 'fallen woman'. They are not accepted as being of equal status to other women and are often in exploitative relationships with their *rasika*. Yet, the *nāchnī nāch* and the *nāchnī shalyā jhūmūr* reveal an aspect of folk/tribal society that is rarely discussed in scholarly literature. Surajit Sinha (1995), who is one of the few scholars who has written about the development of a feudal aristocracy among the Bhumij, talks about the sense of decadence that pervaded the Barabhum *rājbārī* (royal family). Barabhum *rāj*, now a part of Purulia district, was formerly a state ruled by Bhumij *zamindārs*. These *zamindārs* claimed the ritual status of Rajput kshatriyas and have an origin myth that accounts for their presence in Chota Nagpur. However, they still maintain ritual links with their fellow tribesmen.

Sinha does not discuss this, but it is obvious that self-consciously aesthetic forms like the *nāchnī shalyā jhūmūr* and the *chhó* dance develop under the patronage of tribal *zamindārs*. Chakravarti (2001) who, as I have already said, is one of the few folklorists who establish a connection between the *nāchnī nāch* and *zamindāri* culture, is somewhat ambivalent about the status of the latter vis-à-vis the folk culture of this region. In the introduction to his book *Nachni. The Dancing Girls of Rural Bengal*, he talks about the role of *zamindārs* in preserving this dance form. However, further on in the book, he says that the *zamindārs* only turned to the *nāchnīs* when they became impoverished and could no longer afford the entertainment offered by the *bāijīs*. He presents the *zamindārs* as outsiders to folk/tribal culture and the *nāchnī shalyā jhūmūr* as a crude version of the *ṭhumrī*, but one that exists before the coming of the *zamindārs* and the development of *bāijī* culture. I quote:

> There are two streams in Nachni-Nritya. One is known as 'Khemti Naach' (the dance is performed on Khemta-Tala or Arr- Khemta) when the next one is called Mota-Tala – which has a longer rhythm and a slower one. The second one is traditional since an artist has to perform some fundamental principles of dance before the actual commencement of the performance.... Factually 'Mota Tala' is couched in sixteen matras (or rhythm) which is also known as 'Tritala'. When this 'Tala' is played in other songs and tune up in six or eight matras we assign it as Dadra, Kaharaba Tala" (2001: 28).

Manuel says that *dādrā* and *kaharvā* are supposed to be derived from folk *tālas* that were adopted by *ṭhumrī* singers. In fact, an examination of the *ṭhumrī* genre may offer insights for the understanding of the *jhūmūr*. Manuel, in an account of the history of the *ṭhumrī* genre says that courtesans were a "major conduit for the exchange of musical ideas and stylistic features between urban classical and the regional folk cultures" (1989: 75). The ambience of the *kóṭhā*, in which it takes it developed form, is supposed to have given it a quality of decadent eroticism. It is not clear in Manuel's account whether this is because of the dominance of the feminine voice in *ṭhumrī*, its roots in folk music or the 'decadent' culture of the Lucknow court that is responsible for the overwhelmingly erotic mood of this genre. Each one of these 'explanations' co-exists with the others forming a cluster of motifs that are used to make sense of a form that 'disorders' the world of Indian classical music (Rao 2000). Vidya Rao, a scholar of the *ṭhumrī* form and a singer herself, says that it developed through the interactions of *déśī* (folk) voices with *mārgi* (classical) *sangeet*. It came to be heard as *mārgi* and courtly rather than as *déśī* music of the household and village, the lifecycle and calendrical rites.

The *jhūmūr* also acquires its distinctive form in the confluence of *déśī* and *mārgi* currents. As we have seen, it has a duel existence – as part of the ritual calendar and as an autonomous art form. The love between Radha and Krishna that is a dominant theme in *jhūmūr* songs gives it a sensual flavour. But unlike the *ṭhumrī* perhaps, it co-exists with other musical forms that are more explicitly erotic. In comparison to certain *jawa geet* exclusively sung by women, *jhūmūrs* are more stylised. In the words of Rao then, how is the *jhūmūr* to be heard? It is thought to be a cultivated form, but many of the men that I knew in Chorida village could sing it. In fact, men of the Dom and Ghasi *jātī* (two of the lowest castes in the village) said that it came naturally to them. Women, unless they have acquired musical training as *nāchnīs*, do not sing *jhūmūrs*. It is called a masculine genre even though the voice embodied in it is often femimine. When I lived in Chorida I discovered that some women did in fact sing *jhūmūrs* though never in the presence of men. I wonder if the taboos associated with the *nāchnī* has anything to do with this prohibition? Or the answer may lie at a deeper level. In Indian mythology, the feminine voice is often associated with subversion (Das 1998). The *jhūmūr* is a musical form that subverts or problematizes the lens of binarism through which scholars often view folk culture. Thus oppositions such as male versus female expressive genres or folk versus classical tradition, are caught up in a creative tension within the *jhūmūr* form and by extension in the writings of the folklorists themselves.

NOTES

1. Since the time when I was doing fieldwork in Purulia, the Government of West Bengal has taken an active interest in fostering some of these 'dying' forms. I am not sure to what extent they have been successful in reviving them at the village level.
2. The *kobiwālās'* performance involved an exchange of repartee in the form of song. Banerjee (1989) describes the songs themselves as *jhūmūrs*.
3. Banerjee (1989) describes the *khemṭā* as a dance with swinging steps, flashing limbs and swaying hip movements. He contrasts this form of dance with the *nautch* of the North Indian *bāi* dancers whose movements were much slower.
4. The italics are in the original text.
5. This period, according to him, begins after the death of Ramprasad Sen (ca. 1718-1775) who pioneered the genre of Shakta *padāvali* and Ramnidhi Gupta or Nidhu babu (1741-1839) who brought the musical form known as *ṭappa* from the Panjab and gave it a uniquely Bengali coloration. Nidhu babu's compositions, Chakraborty says, mark the beginning of the Bengali renaissance in music. The *padāvali* is a form of Bhakti poetry that first developed in Bengal in the fifteenth century as a form of devotion to Krishna. Three hundred years later its influence spread to the worship of Bengal's goddesses as well, especially to Kali and Uma (cf. McDermott 2001).

6. In the village in which I did field work, the *jhūmūr* genre was supposed to be a male preserve. Women only sang Bhadu and Tushu songs, apart from the ritual chants and special ditties that are prescribed as part of ritual performance. I suppose this was because women who do sing *jhūmūrs* are *nāchnīs* and are outside the circumscribed social world of most women. There is, however, one class of *jhūmūr* that is sung by women – the *bhāduriā jhūmūr*. Women who work in the fields, transplanting paddy in the rainy season sing *bhāduriā jhūmūr* songs. However, this is usually not done in the presence of men. Transplanting paddy is exclusively women's work and women are the only humans present in the fields when they sing. Bhaduria *jhūmūr* songs have also become a form of high art and are sung by *nāchnīs* as well (Chatterji 1987). Bhattacharya (1965) says that *jhūmūrs*, even when sung by *nāchnīs*, are composed by men, which makes it a largely masculine form.
7. Dutt incorporated folk dances into the Bratachari Movement. This was a movement that he started in 1934 for the renewal of "New Life, of citizenship, social service, work and joy, national and international fellowship..." (1954: 7-8). It had as its goal the development of the physical and moral capabilities of the youth through the medium of folk culture.
8. As Dutt (1954) says, the eleventh century marks the end of the Sena period. The Pala and Sena dynasties were significant in that they left their signature on the early civilization of what is now Bengal.
9. Dutt, himself, preferred to take the *Raibeshe* and *Dhali* dances as models for the Bratachari movement because of their warlike nature rather than the *jhūmūr*, in spite of his belief that the chain *jhūmūr* fostered solidarity and democracy.
10. See the first chapter for a demonstration of the point.
11. The *Padāvali kīrtana* was popularised by the followers of Chaitanya Mahaprabhu in the fifteenth century. As further proof of the antiquity of the *Shri Krishna Kīrtana*, the scholars say that there is textual evidence that Chaitanya used to have it sung to him (B. Chattopadhya 2001).
12. They are, according to Sinha (1995), also one of the few tribal groups in central India that have resisted the pull of state formation and 'Rajputisation'.
13. This has been translated as *The Structure of Hindu Society* (1975) by Andre Beteille.
14. There is a long history to this. Rabindranath Tagore and Satyajit Ray, the filmmaker, are two of the more famous Bengali intellectuals who have used the Santhals as a symbol of cultural alterity to critically reflect on their own middle- class Bengali ethos.
15. My use of the male voice is deliberate here. Apart from specific periods in the work cycle and significant exceptions like the *nāchnī*, the *jhūmūr* is largely the preserve of men (Chatterji 1998).

16. The *karam pūjā* is performed by low castes and tribal groups in Purulia, in the month of September or October. Informants said that it was a kind of *shasṭi pūjā* performed by women for the welfare of their brothers. However unlike the *shasṭi pūjās* that are performed within domestic space at various times of the year, *karam pūjā* is a public ritual and received royal patronage in Purulia.
17. The *rasika* is one who is a connoisseur of the form. The *rasika,* in Purulia, usually 'keeps' the *nāchnī*/s, trains them to sing and dance and performs with them.
18. There is an old tradition of essentialising tribal cultures in terms of an erotic or sensuous sentiment (Hardy 1983, Mahato 2001).
19. By 'folk' he means rural and region specific.

4

Feminine Figures in Narrative Forms

The figure of the woman, whether a goddess like Bhadu or the *nāchnī*, always has the potential to subvert received systems of classifications. In this chapter I explore the subversive potential of the feminine voice and its significance for our understanding of folk culture. Feminist scholars have shown that it is the position that women occupy within structures of patriarchy and yet not be totally incorporated within them that gives the feminine voice its symbolic charge (Trawick 1990, Das 1998, Raheja and Gold 1996). But this voice is also shaped by the genres in which it is embedded. The narrative genres in which folklore themes are couched, whether they achieve resolution and have a definite end or are open-ended – all these structural features contribute to the form that stories take and limit the kinds of questions that can be asked in the narrative. The focus on genre also helps to problematise a conception of folk culture that is based on a notion of unanimous community (Coomaraswamy 1956). Particular genres offer specific perspectives on the world and folk artists or narrators explicitly choose from the repertoire of genres available in their cultures.

Structures of patriarchy embedded within intracommunity relations are problematised by foregrounding gender divisions that are sometimes thought to cut across and even subvert traditional patterns of community formation. Thus Flueckiger (1996) shows how gendered claims over particular genres may create alternate forms of community defined on the basis of their performative traditions. In a some what different vein Raheja and Gold (1994) problematise the notion of domestic community through a study of women's songs that subvert patriarchal relationships within the kinship domain. In a sensitive essay on male and female voices in the *Ramacharitamanasa*, Veena Das (1998) characterises the feminine voice as one of interrogation. Goddesses like Sati, Parvati and even Sita are depicted as figures who at crucial moments in the narrative, doubt the authoritative representation of divine truth and are then punished for this. Yet as Das recounts, the questions remain and the figures of these goddesses become the archetypal listeners whose interventions in the text allow the narrative to move forward. Thus the answer to a question always takes the form of an additional story. For instance, take the episode in the *Ramacharitamanasa* in which Shiva and Sati encounter Rama in exile in the Dandaka forest. Rama is distraught with grief at the loss of his beloved Sita, just as any ordinary man would be if separated from a much loved wife. However, Shiva knows that Rama is an *avatāra* (incarnation) of Vishnu and bows before him. Sita, however, is suspicious of Rama's divinity and to allay her doubt Shiva tells her the story of Rama's birth and of the other incarnations of Vishnu. The fact that Sati is not convinced by the story and decides to put Rama to the test by appearing before him in the guise of Sita is important for the form that the narrative takes, even though a fuller discussion on this is beyond the scope of this chapter (Das 1998). Suffice it to say that in this narrative, doubt becomes the mode of listening. Figures like Sati give human beings, "a method of listening to the narrative of the divine – not as an embodiment of absolute truth but as subject to the doubt of the listener" (Das 1998: 71). I consider Das's work important because it extrapolates from the narrative to explore questions regarding truth and skepticism in the human world. Sacred stories, in many Indian traditions, are considered to have an intimate relationship with everyday life. In my own work I have shown how relations of intimacy between ordinary, flesh and blood persons and characters in such sacred stories are established in the mode of listening (Chatterji 1987). Thus, during my fieldwork in a village in Purulia, when a narration of a sacred text took place (*pāṭḥ*) the listeners were made part of the story. For example, at a reading of the *Mahabharata*, Abhimanyu's wedding was celebrated with a traditional wedding feast and all the listeners were treated as *bārātīs* (part of the bridegroom's procession).

Conditions of listening are always premised on particular conceptions of voice (Chatterji 1998). Our ability to listen to a voice, or conversely turning our attention away from a voice, may reflect centrally on our desire or need to establish relations of intimacy with another person. But what do I mean by voice here? Das (2006) uses the concept of voice to examine issues of reflexivity and creativity in culture and in the domain of everyday life. She questions the anthropological view of culture that formulates it as obedience to a set of normative rules and procedures. Instead she foregrounds the process by which one may come "to a sense of shared culture" by finding a voice within it (Das 2006).

In an earlier work on life stories I have tried to show how women whose lives rarely form part of public discourse use poetic and musical forms that are tabooed to them to speak of personal events that would otherwise be silenced (Chatterji 2002). Men on the contrary, who are allowed culturally prescribed ways of expressing personal sentiment are silent. Thus, in the part of Purulia where I did my fieldwork, songs in the *jhūmūr* genre that reflect the *bhakti* mood are said to be the preserve of men[1]. Women sometimes compose in this form even though they cannot sing them in public, because it allows for the expression of personal emotion, of love and conjugal emotion, thinly veiled in the love relationship between Radha and Krishna. One of my women friends in the village where I did my fieldwork sang a *jhūmūr* song for me that she had composed about her own life in conditions of absolute secrecy. I only came to know that she was a gifted composer towards the end of my stay in the village. Another friend told me about this special song which she could not sing for my tape recorder because it was a *jhūmūr*. However she did let me tape it, as a parting gift, but we had to go to a deserted field in the middle of the afternoon, out of the hearing of any villager especially a male. It is not as if women cannot compose or sing in the *jhūmūr* form. As I have just shown, they sometimes do, but in a largely oral tradition not to be able to sing a song in the presence of others is almost as bad as not being allowed to sing at all. In an earlier work (Chatterji 2002) I have discussed questions relating to biography and voice in greater detail. I have argued that even though the composers of *jhūmūr* songs are largely men, the connection between the formulaic style of expressing sentiment and personal emotion is so elliptical that it becomes difficult to read the private experiences that may have been the impulse behind such compositions.

I have argued that it is because women are never fully incorporated into the normative structures of their societies that subversion becomes an archetypal feminine activity. However, such an argument can come dangerously close to a kind of sociological reductionism unless I can demonstrate the symbolic potential that feminine figures have in the social imaginary that make such subversion possible. To this end I will explore the feminine images portrayed in some of the narrative traditions of Purulia, in the hope that they will throw light on contradictions and tensions within a seemingly coherent cultural tradition. (Also by comparing three different narrative traditions I can draw attention to the fact that the aesthetic dimension of cultural form is part of folk creativity and not just a contribution of the literary imagination of the metropole. A focus on genre reconfigures folk culture as the space of intellection.)

The first narrative that I take up for discussion is a *kahānī* (stories that are made up – pronounced *kohonī* in the local language). *Kahāni* is located in fictional time, a time that is closed in on itself. It is opposed to *kathā* (sacred story or truth that is uttered – pronounced – *kauthā*). The events that are narrated as *kathā* are seen as occurring in real time although in past *yugas*. They posit causal relationships between events that occurred in the archetypal past and the present state of the world. 'Causality', however, may not be the most appropriate term to describe the *līlā* (divine play) within which this relationship is inscribed. *Jān kahānī* (riddle), the third form of narrative that I describe, foregrounds this aspect of *kathā* though not always in a mode of celebration. The riddle that I present for discussion reveals the dark side of play.

THE KAHĀNĪ

A merchant had only one son whose wife came from a very distant land. She was extremely wise and knew the languages of all the beasts and birds in the forest. The merchant's house was near the river. One night a corpse laden with jewels floated by. A jackal saw it from the river bank and asked the woman to haul it out, so that it could eat it. It told her that she could keep the jewels. She bit the corpse's swollen finger to remove a precious ring that had got stuck on it. Her husband saw her and thought that she was a demoness eating human flesh. He told his father this, and they decided to abandon her in the forest. The woman's husband told her that he was taking her to her father's house. When they reached the forest they saw a large toad sitting in the middle of the path. It said that a snake was waiting to eat it. If they could kill the snake it would give them seven pearls – each worth the wealth of seven kings. The wife made her husband, the merchant's son, kill the snake and took the pearls. He was very impressed with her knowledge and realised his mistake. He took her home, left her there and went out to work. The merchant, the father-in-law saw her in the house alone and thought that she had killed his son, her husband. He cut off her head before she could tell him about her special gifts and was stricken with remorse when the truth was revealed to him.

Stories within the *kahānī* genre typically dramatise the journey of the self – from a state of imperfection that is riddled with contradiction to a higher state in which these contradictions have been resolved. This qualitative movement is portrayed spatially as a journey undertaken by the hero that serves to mediate between the two states of being. In this story, the dichotomy between culture and nature is used to represent the two states of being.

The categories of nature and culture form the analytical axis for most structuralist descriptions of the narrative universe (Levi Strauss 1970, Greimas 1971). However, the topographical space of the narratives that are analysed in terms of nature and culture looks somewhat different if gender is used to orient the texts. Thus, in the story recounted here culture, which is the domain of masculinity, is not thought of as sacred as would be the case in the narratives examined by Levi Strauss. Instead it is the familiar and routinised world that the self inhabits. It is also the realm of fear and ignorance. It represents a state of imperfect communication and inadequate knowledge. Nature is the realm of potential, the giver of abundance to those who have the ability to communicate with her. It is a place of mystery, an other that is perceived as a threat to the world of the self. It is also the realm of femininity. (For Levi Strauss, on the other hand, nature is the domain of anti-culture.) Culture is the domain of order within which the darker aspects of nature are hierarchically encompassed and subdued.)

The tragedy that results from a misunderstanding of the relationship between the other and the self is the key theme of the story. Like most stories in the genre of *kahānī*, this story uses a critical event to mark a disjunction in the sequence of episodes, such that they can be clearly demarcated into a 'before' – the initial state of imperfection and an 'after' – the final state of perfection. However, this story is unusual in that the initial state of imperfect communication instead of providing an impetus for the progression to a higher state of being, becomes a block against it. The death of the wise woman, the potential mediator between the two states, is an absurd (i.e. meaningless) death that leads to a permanent separation between the before and the after, a negative resolution with no possibility of redemption for human culture.

THE KATHA

The story that I describe here is a *vrata kathā* (pronounced *brótó kauthā* in Bangla), narrated as part of the *Ganesh chóṭ pūjā*, a ritual performed largely by women, on the fourth day of the bright half of the month of *Kārtik* (mid–October to mid–November).

Parvati and Shiva came down to earth to see if their son Ganesha's *pūjā* was being performed. In their wanderings on earth, Parvati saw a blind man and took pity on his affliction. She asked Shiva to help him but Shiva replied that it was in the man's fate to be blind and he could do nothing to change that. He then added that he did not travel with women as a rule precisely for this reason. They insisted on interfering in matters that were beyond their concern. But Parvati persisted, and when all else failed she insisted on leaving a pot full of money in the blind man's path. The blind man could not see the pot and passed it by. Shiva turned to his wife and said that his utterance had been confirmed – the blind man's fate, determined by his *karma* from previous births, did not allow him to benefit from unexpected good fortune.

After walking in silence for some time, Shiva and Parvati heard sounds of mourning coming from a house that seemed to be decorated as for a wedding. Parvati, her curiosity aroused by this paradoxical situation, took on the guise of an old Brahmin woman and went into the house to investigate. She discovered that the bridegroom had died on his wedding day. She returned to Shiva, who reluctantly agreed to help her. He told her to find a broken brick. Parvati saw many brick kilns, with new bricks but she could not find a broken brick. Again Shiva warned her that the boy was fated to die, it was written on his forehead (*kaupāl*). Parvati finally managed to find a broken brick. She sprinkled brick dust on the boy's forehead and he became alive. Parvati instructed the women in the household on the virtues of the *Ganesh chót pūjā* and departed with an increasingly irascible Shiva.

They then saw a man unsuccessfully trying to milk a cow that kept kicking him. The cow refused to be milked by human hands. Disguised once again as an old Brahmin woman, Parvati told the man that the cow would become docile if he performed the *Ganesh chót pūjā*. Then she saw a tree that bore insect-ridden fruit. She promised the owner that insects would no longer attack the tree if he performed the *pūjā*. After a while, a terrible storm arose. Shiva and Parvati were separated. Shiva returned to his abode in the Kailash mountain. Parvati fell into a ditch near a potter's house. The potter had just returned home and he called out his daughter, who was also named Parvati, to relieve him of his load of clay. Parvati (the goddess) answered and took his load from him. When he came into the house he saw two Parvatis. The goddess told him that she too was his daughter and had come to visit him. The day of *Ganesh chóṭ pūjā* came. Parvati, the goddess, asked for a little sun baked rice (*ālό chāl*) to make sweets (*pūā*) for the *pūjā*. The old potter was poor and could not afford to buy very much. But once Parvati started to cook, there seemed to be a never-ending supply of sweets. Shiva came with their two sons Ganesha and Kartikya to see her. Shiva's bull and Parvati's, perhaps I should say Durga's, lion sat at the door–way of the kitchen while the goddess fed her family. The potter came upon the bull and the lion and cried out to his 'daughter' to save herself. Shiva left hastily with the family and Parvati told the old man that she would have to return to her husband.

The potter wanted to give Parvati a new *sāri* before she left. But he had only eight *annas* in the house. With this small amount he went to a shop and with some trepidation showed the money to the shopkeeper. The shopkeeper showed him an expensive silk *sārī*. The potter left the shop hastily, in great embarrassment. However, the same thing happened in the next shop he went to and the one after that. Finally, in the tenth shop that he went to, he told the shopkeeper that he wanted a *sārī* that was worth eight *annas* only.

The shopkeeper offered him a beautiful silk *sārī* and said that its price was eight *annas*. Parvati (Durga) put on the *sārī* and called out to the potter, after carefully hiding the lion behind her. She showed him her ten-armed form and blessed him with untold wealth. She said that henceforth all his pots would turn to gold. The potter hastily asked her to revoke the boon (*var* or *baur*) and asked instead, for pots that would break at the touch of a human hand. Gold pots, he said, were bought only once in a lifetime while fragile clay pots were bought every day.

In this story, Parvati/Durga is portrayed as a kind-hearted woman who interferes with the decrees of fate, not merely out of self–interest to establish the *Ganesh chót pūjā*, but out of a genuine concern for the well being of her devotees. Shiva is the dispassionate and detached observer, far removed from the world of man, the upholder of the law of *karma*. Together, they represent the two aspects of the divine – the impartial observer cruel in his detachment, watching the *līlā* of his own creations dispassionately, and the benevolent mother concerned with the welfare of her children. It has to be remembered that the *vrata* kathās, stories narrated in the course of performing rituals, are used exclusively by women. In this story we can see that Shiva and Parvati/Durga represent the different aspects of the divine as seen from the opposing perspectives of men and women. Parvati/Durga is seen as embodying the feminine principle of nuture and care, and Shiva as embodying the masculine principle – the impartial upholder of the law of *karma*. It is not as if stories about masculine deities related by men do not establish relations on the human plane. The role of the *avatāras*, after all, is precisely that of succour and the relief of human society from the evils that beset it. But the relief that the *avatāras* offer is at a much more impersonal level – from the archetypal demons that embody the destructive aspects of society or like Sri Chaitanya they offer succour in the form of *bhakti*, a submerging of the individual personality into Godhead and a detachment from the more mundane goals of society. The *vrata kathās*, in contrast, emphasise the states of material well being and portray them as the signs of spiritual worth, which are embodied in the correct performance of the rituals and prescriptions expected of the householder.

This narrative unlike the *kahānī* recounted earlier lacks a definite resolution. The potter's comical though pragmatic response to the goddesses first boon – "Let me have pots of clay that break at the touch rather than pots of gold so that I earn everyday", – with which this story ends, gives the narrative an open – ended quality, one that mimics life itself.[2] Kathās not only tell us why the world is as it is, their sacred quality comes as much from the way they replicate narratives of everyday life. But what kind of resolution does the first story, a *kahānī*, have? Unlike most of the *kahānīs* in my collection – it has a negative resolution – it is only at the moment of death that the truth that the heroine represents is revealed. The theme of sacrificial death and its relation to the spoken word in its many forms – to sayings, commands and assertions – is the subject of the last narrative that I will take up for discussion.

JĀN KAHĀNĪ

Jān kahānīs (riddles) – literally, 'the story to be known' or the 'story whose answer is to be known' – is thought to be a form of inspired speech in Purulia. Fundamental social values are questioned in the form of a play with words. Thus,

Kautó nām dhauré kintū tīnī śótī

(This could mean either that she bares so many names but is nevertheless a *sati* (virtuous woman); or that her name is borne by so many, i.e. in their voices or in their speech, but she is *sati* (virtuous)/ Sati (the Goddess))

pītār bakké té dāé jībón āhūtī

(At her father's saying/command (*vākya*) she give her life to the sacrifice, i.e. immolates herself in the sacred fire.)

The answer is Daksha's daughter Sati, also described as truth personified, who throws herself into the sacrificial fire in her father's house – to avenge the insult to her husband, the god Shiva who had not been invited to the great *yagya* that Daksha had organised (Monier Williams 1899).

The play on the name – Sati, the Mother Goddess, *sati*, a feminine attribute – the good wife, made virtuous through the act of self immolation (*sati*) is counterposed with another kind of word play, again focused on the name. The fact that the Mother Goddess is known by many names, since no single name is adequate in capturing her manifold attributes, is counterposed by the suggestion that her name is uttered by many (men). Can a woman whose name is taken by so many men – (women do not officially have voices)- be chaste? This question often rhetorically prefigures narrations about Draupadi – the wife of the five Pandava brothers and key figure in the epic narrative, the *Mahabharata*. Various episodes in Draupadi's previous births are then recounted to explain how she comes to be the wife of five men simultaneously, without losing her womanly virtue. The riddle also plays with the theme of sacrifice. In an important work on the vedic sacrifice, the French Indologist Charles Malamoud (1989) likens *yajña*, the essential part of the sacrificial ceremony, to the male body.[3] But speech (*vac*) that accompanies *yajña* is feminine. As a feminine figure speech is always plural. Thus speech is twofold, that is fickle, capable of being both truth and falsehood. He says that the assemblage of sacred objects and practices can be organised into male and female pairs in which the male is always singular and the female plural.

Thus this riddle follows the structure of the sacrifice, as delineated by Malamoud – conjoining speech and sacrifice, life and death. Speech as truth – as the injunction of the Father – is one. But speech in the form of the many names of the mother goddess is multiple, reflecting the shades of life itself. As the sacrificial victim, Sati also becomes many. In death she is fragmented, her body parts are scattered across the land creating sacred "crossings" (*tīrthas*) where the divine realm intersects with the profane world. Riddles play with the limits of meaning without actually subverting the moral order in which they are embedded. Yet precisely because they are a form of play they point to fissures or contradictions in the moral order.

In an earlier work (cf. Chatterji 1987) I have explored the ways in which different narrative traditions appeal to different regions of the self in its relation to the social world. In this chapter I want to explore this idea in a somewhat different way. The figure of the woman that I have chosen to depict emerges only across different narrative forms that I have described – she is not captured fully in any one of them. It is as if the silences imposed by the limits of any one form call upon the other narrative forms to speak out. Is there something about the symbolic potential of womanhood that rejects the constraint of form itself?

Trawick (1990) quoting Kristeva says that all languages contain conventional knowledge about the ontological status of the world, about how the world is supposed to be. However, as with all conventions, their status is arbitrary, and it is the force of social authority that make them seem true. In the narratives recounted here the force of authority as well as its interrogation, the revelation of its arbitrary nature is represented anthropomorphically through male and female figures. If the figure of authority, the voice that pronounces the law (*dharma*) is masculine as the stories recounted here show, either in the figure of Shiva who pronounces the law or Daksha who commands the sacrifice, then it is the feminine figure, Durga who challenges this law or Sati who overturns the sacrifice – performed in anger by her father in a manner that is both exclusionary and unjust – in sorrow by immolating herself. Sati, like Durga represents the voice of skepticism vis–à–vis sacred truth. She voices another kind of truth set in the mode of interrogation and she does so from the region of death.

The motif of death occurs in all three narratives. Sometimes as a resolution to he story as in the first case, or in a playful mood, as a juxtaposition of laughter and sorrow as in the second story. Here death is overturned not so much as a heroic event but rather as something slightly ironic – Shiva is portrayed as a husband whose patience is stretched to the limit and who finally gives in to his wife's willful and persistent demands. Death, in the third narrative is the most dramatic and the most resolute – death as the effect of an assertion or command, the voice of patriarchy. Sati, disobeys the voice of patriarchy and insists on going where she is not invited. However, if we unpack the sequence of events that lead to Sati's supposed suicide, it reveals another, more complex structure, made up of a weave of different stories. In the *Adhyatma Ramayana* (cf. Raghavan 1980) it is said that the goddess was witness to Rama's anguish when he was bereft of his beloved wife Sita. She turned to Shiva, her consort, and asked him if this was the same Rama, the all – knowing *avatāra* of Vishnu who was never separated from his wife, the goddess Lakshmi, or was this another, perhaps human, Rama? The story unfolds from this question, in the voice of Shiva who tells his wife how Rama comes to occupy human form. However, from that time onwards, Shiva mentally repudiated the goddess, in sorrow rather than anger because her doubts showed her to be imperfect. It is the slow realisation of this that led her to kill herself. However, because her death replicates the structure of the sacrifice she is reborn and attains Shiva as husband once again.

This story captures the many voices of male authority – the divine law embodied in the voice of the husband (Shiva) and the irrascable, though no less powerful voice of the father (Daksha). By juxtaposing the two voices through the figure of female death, the arbitrary, even willful nature of the supposedly dispassionate, authoritative voice is revealed. The moment of death is always extremely important, not just in the lives of individuals but in the lives of communities as well. Death is the time when communities have to confront difficult truths that are normally hidden in everyday life. Death when cast in feminine form is even more difficult. The moment of death casts its shadow on the moment of birth. Some so called pre-modern societies characterise the transition between life and death as the "laughing threshold" (Propp 1984:133). "Folkloric laughter" is thought to be tied to the temporal rhythms of pre-modern societies. It articulates the agricultural seasons of village life, marking the gap between life and death, between lack and abundance, but in the process filling this gap with its own particular signature – signaling not an absence but the presence of hope and the anticipation of regeneration. However, as these three narratives show folk laughter is a complex phenomenon and cannot be thought of merely as a representation of collective life (Chatterji 1998). In all these narratives, the woman – the archetypal life–giver – is also the voice of skepticism, a skepticism that is associated with death. It is as if the woman's voice, that is, the voice of doubt, is also associated with the birth of community. Death expressed through the voice of skepticism allows community to reflect on itself – in short, to be reborn.

NOTES

1. Of course, this statement is also reflective of the condition of patriarchy because it does not take into account the figure of the *nāchnī* or professional dancer who is accomplished in the singing of *jhūmūr* songs nor that of the women who labour in the fields and have the tradition of singing *bhāduriā jhūmūrs* while they transplant paddy in the monsoon season. Both these categories of women actually do sing in public, they are also paid for the work they do which puts them in a somewhat liminal position vis–à–vis the normative female roles of wife and mother.

2. Interestingly, the goddess is able to revoke the first boon. Divine utterance does not have an irrevocable quality in this story.
3. This is the culminating moment at which the victim is put to death.

5

Conclusion : Folklore and Border Crossings

In Bengal 'folk culture' emerges in the conjunction between an emerging literary imagination and a nationalist discourse. Some of the early folklorists like Dinesh Chandra Sen and Dakshinaranjan Mitra Mazumdar collected folk stories as part of a nationalist endeavour to demonstrate that Bengal did have a vibrant indigenous literature.[1] Gurusaday Dutt, inspired by the folk dance movement in England, established institutions for folk dance in Calcutta and it became an intrinsic part of the *Bratachari* movement (Chatterji 2003).[2]

In post-Independence India, the nationalist ideology of 'unity in diversity' supported the articulation of autonomous regional cultures, albeit within a unified pan-Indian frame. 'Traditional' forms of cultural expression came to represent regional identity such that Bharat Natyam became the classical dance form best suited to express the cultural ethos of Tamil Nadu, Kathakali of Kerala and so on (Swapna Sundari 2005). If this is the case what happens to cultural zones that cut across regional borders – to forms like the *chhó* and the *jhūmūr* that are appropriated by more than one state? Recent attempts to appropriate cultural forms from border regions like Purulia are not merely political exercises initiated by state governments. Purulia has become part of the literary imagination of Bengal via the circulation of folkloric discourse.[3] The circulation of folkloric representations have led to the emergence of a new social imaginary and to the formation of new publics to whom these cultural forms are now addressed.

Purulia, as the site of folk expressivity, becomes exoticised in the process. However, as I have tried to show, the constitution of cultural alterety involves a complex process involving multiple and overlapping frames. Representations of Purulia through the *chhó* that conceive of it as Bengal's tribal other are different from representations generated through Bhadu and Tushu songs or through the figure of the *nāchnī*. Bhadu and Tushu songs produce the alter as woman – a symbol of universal cultural subalterneity. This representation is subverted by the *nāchnī* and by her contribution to the development of the *jhūmūr* genre. Most scholars would agree that the cultures of the local courts in regions like Purulia in which the institution of the *nāchnī* and *rasika* flourished was crucial for the development of the *jhūmūr*. Yet even though they consider the *jhūmūr* as part of the folk music of Purulia they find it more difficult to include the institution of the *nāchnī* or even the *nāchnī nāch* as part of its folk culture.

This brings me to an important issue that is still not adequately thematised in the writings on folklore – that is, the contribution of the state in the production of locality (Appadurai 1997). The folk culture of Purulia is produced through a specific conjunction between cultural creativity and political domination. It cannot be seen apart from the process of state formation in tribal Central India that has been studied by scholars like Surajit Sinha (1995) – an aspect that I have addressed in the introduction. In this chapter I only want to emphasise on the fact that folklore is a historical phenomenon as it emerges in societies that are open to the forces of change. But more importantly the study of folklore is a historical phenomenon. But before I discuss this in greater detail it is necessary to consider just how Purulia emerges as a folklore region.

EMERGENT EVENTS

To address the question of how Purulia becomes a folklore region I discuss two historical moments in the history of Bengal. These are the Swadeshi (Self-Rule) Movement of 1905-1910 and the Partition of India in 1947. Both these events are of great significance in understanding the articulation of the discipline of folklore with the growth of cultural nationalism. I do not mean to suggest that there is a causal relation or a chronological association between these historical moments and the development of the discipline of folklore. Instead, I consider these two moments as 'emergent events'. As Mead said, events that stick out from the flow of time have the capacity of reconceptualising our notions of past and future (Joas 1985). I also take from Foucault the idea that the relationship between 'events' and other things that happen is one of juxtaposition rather than correlation. Events are contingent to the extent that the 'conditions of possibility' that they give rise to are usually 'unintended consequences' – that is, a combination of circumstances in seemingly disconnected fields that give rise to a certain outcome (Hunt and Wickham 1994, Foucault 1977). However these events are originary to the extent that they reveal an aspect of history that may have otherwise remained in the realm of the virtual (Deleuze 1991).

The immediate impulse that sparked off the nationalist upsurge of 1905-1910 in Bengal, better known as the Swadeshi movement, was the plan to partition the province of Bengal.[4] The rationale for the partition was purportedly administrative. Bengal was thought to be too large a province to govern efficiently. However there were also political reasons for this move, such as the threat of a burgeoning national movement that had begun in the late nineteenth century (Sarkar 1973). What is interesting from the point of view of this work is that it is during this period that folklore is used for the first time as a means of political mobilisation. Thus new folk songs were composed by nationalist poets like Rabindranath Tagore to spread the idea of *swadeshi* and traditional institutions like the *melā* (fair) were used to propagate the movement. Even though the first folklore collections in Bengal date back to the nineteenth century, The Swadeshi movement gave these endeavours a new meaning.[5] They used these folklore collections to establish that there was "a common culture at the village level based on an amalgam of Hindu, Buddhist, Muslim and primitive folk elements" (Sarkar 1973: 23).[6] Also by using traditional institutions in new ways they helped to develop new techniques of transmission and forms of folklore that were later adopted by organisations with very different ideologies. The cultural movement led by the communists in the early 1940s such as the Indian People's Theatre Association (IPTA), also encouraged the creation of new popular and folk forms that could be used to propagate their political ideology. The IPTA movement has indirect significance for the region that we have been discussing. It tried to incorporate ideas taken from socialist realism into folk and popular genres. Thus, it was because of their performances in rural India that contemporary political events like the Great Bengal famine of 1943 gave rise to numerous folk songs (see appendix 2).[7] In Purulia it may have also encouraged the use of folk songs for political mobilisation at the time of the linguistic re-organisation of states after independence. In this way the IPTA movement actively fostered the idea of a generic 'Indianness' that became the dominant orientation of the state in its role as patron of the arts (Pradhan 1979). A particular articulation of the category of 'folk' was beginning to emerge through the juxtaposition of contradictory representations that stressed both regional distinctiveness and generic Indianness.

Independence and the partition of the sub-continent in 1947 mark another important moment in the history of Bengali folklore scholarship. East Bengal, the terrain on which much of the folkloric activity occurred, became a part of Pakistan. Even though Purulia was incorporated into West Bengal only in 1956 as part of the move to re-organise states on the basis of common language – its emergence as a folklore region must be attributed to the partition of India. Nationalist folklorists had looked to East Bengal, with its large Muslim peasant population, for a syncretic and secular folk culture that could be used as a counter-representation to the image of a spiritual and other-worldly India propounded by the Orientalists (Sarkar 1985).[8] In East Bengal they found a composite, even hybrid culture composed of an amalgam of Hindu and Muslim strands – combining a generic Indianness and a regional distinctiveness.[9]

Purulia was discovered as a folklore region in the early 1960s. Before this the only time it caught the attention of the public was during the Tushu Satyagraha – the movement to separate Purulia from Bihar and incorporate it in West Bengal (Sinha 1974). Purulia's folk songs were considered to be subversive by the Bihar Government and the public singing of Tushu folk songs was banned, being perceived as a threat to the political autonomy of the state. As we shall see in the sections that follow, many of the issues that concerned the early folklorists writing from the vantage point of the folk culture of East Bengal were transposed on to the terrain of Purulia. This involved a process of translation – from Muslim and Hindu peasant to tribal culture, aided by the fact that the dominant tribal groups have become peasants in Purulia as well, but also a silencing of the distinctive aspects of tribal culture. To understand the process by which this occurred we must return to the nationalist discourse on folklore.

THE FOLK IN RELATION TO AN INDIAN NATIONALIST AESTHETIC

Folklore played a significant role in the reconstitution of tradition in the nationalist discourse in India. However, while it served as an important source of historical reconstruction, there were divergent views on its relationship with the present, with modern Indian society – shaped as it was by the forces of imperialism and colonisation. In this section I shall examine some of the concepts used by prominent nationalist scholars like Ananda Coomaraswamy and Gurusaday Dutt to reconfigure folklore within an essentially 'Indian' discourse. The constitution of a national tradition involves an act of translation by which cultural meanings are addressed to and through an Other (Bhaba 1994). The Other that the Indian nationalists were responding to were the 'colonisers' – the British intellectuals who viewed Indian art and culture through categories of Western aesthetics but also the 'orientalists' whose idealised representations of Indian civilization, provided a prism through which they addressed questions relating to Indian art and culture. The tradition that they were trying to reconstitute had a synthetic even hybrid quality. However, to understand the nature of this hybridity one will have to unravel the different strands in their discourse. Was this tradition discontinuous and would it therefore allow for selective reappropriation or was it unbroken and continuous, unscathed by historical events? For scholars who held to the former view folk culture was a trace of a time gone by and a sign of temporal disruption and for those holding the latter view, it was the source of authentic tradition that continued to exist from pre-historic times.

The process of translation resulted in the destabilisation of the term "folklore", giving it new and unexpected connotations. Thus Coomaraswamy uses an Indian classificatory scheme – the division *ga* (highway) and *deśī* (byway, local) – in his essay on folklore and popular art (Coomaraswamy 1956). However, unlike the Western case, he finds that folk art falls within the category of *mārga* or high art. According to Coomaraswamy universal and eternal values are always embodied through the sacred. Therefore, since Indian folklore speaks exclusively in the voice of the sacred it must necessarily embody universal values. Rather, it is the courtly arts like Mogul miniature painting that deal with worldly and secular themes that must be characterised as *deśī* or parochial.

Coomaraswamy's essay must be viewed in the light of his life-long endeavour to establish a separate and distinct aesthetic tradition in India. He was reacting to colonial representations of Indian art as merely decorative and sensuous and sought to highlight the spiritualism behind the appearance of sensuous form (Guha-Thakurta 1992). As a nationalist he was also deeply interested in the 'Bengal School' painters and their efforts at reconstituting the Indian art tradition. Painters belonging to the Bengal School, like Abanindranath Tagore, were conscious that they were in the process of constituting a national tradition – an aesthetics that could represent the whole of India. They tried to create a synthetic and universal style borrowing elements from different regional styles and techniques, even some from outside India. For example, Abanindranath Tagore adopted the wash technique in watercolour painting from Japan as this enabled him to express the innate spiritualism of the Indian tradition. Thus this technique enabled him to portray indistinct forms in misty grounds, allowing him to express the inner meaning of the images by negating the distinctiveness of material form (Guha-Thakurta 1992). Interestingly Tagore was also interested in folk art. In a book on the folk rituals of Bengal he says that these rituals, which are still performed in rural Bengal, show traces of pre-Aryan, pre-Brahminic culture (Tagore 1919).

Village India, especially the spheres associated with the home and with domesticity are represented as an autonomous inner space in the nationalist discourse. This space continues to exist in modern times untouched by the effects of colonisation. Thus the Indian people are thought to be the inheritors of a discontinuous tradition. Folklore bore the traces of another time. Coomaraswamy says that, "folk memory" serves "the purpose of a sort of ark, in which the wisdom of a former age is carried over (*tiryate*) the period of dissolution..." (1956:139). This wisdom is not necessarily understood by the 'folk' (*jana*) but forms part of their lived tradition.

Folklore and folk culture was thought to have a significant role in the constitution of an Indian aesthetic tradition. However, the nationalist discourse was by no means homogeneous in its conceptualisation of the folk. Gurusaday Dutt, who became interested in the folk culture of Bengal in the course of his work as a colonial administrator, had a perspective on folk culture that was diametrically opposed to that of Coomaraswamy and the Bengal School artists. He did not believe that India had ever had a unified aesthetic tradition. Each region had its own distinctive style and any attempt to create a pan-Indian style would be detrimental to the living cultures still flourishing in the different parts of India. Let me elaborate on his position.

For Dutt (1990) folk culture represented the national culture of Bengal. It was in a relationship of unbroken continuity with pre-Aryan Indian civilization but also managed to absorb the best of Aryan culture. It was able to synthesise both these civilizational streams. However it was only able to express its true significance in certain phases of Bengal's political history. That is when it was freed from the domination of pan-Indian imperial powers viz. the Guptas, Palas and Senas that held sway in Bengal till about the twelfth century. He made a distinction between the aristocratic art tradition that he called the 'patroned *mārga*' (courtly or aristocratic way) and the *sahaja mārga* (the popular and spontaneous way) represented by the work of village artists who created artistic forms within ritual and in the activities of daily life.

Coomaraswamy did not believe that there was a fundamental difference in value between aristocratic and folk art. They were both embedded within the sacred tradition. However it was only the folk who still survived and managed to preserve this tradition in modern India as I have already said. Dutt believed that the sacred realm itself was divided between the institutions shaped by priestly and imperial power and the natural religion of the folk. However, in spite of their differences their perspectives have something in common – the folk, whether defined as a *jana* or "a unanimous community" in Coomaraswamy's terms or as a 'race culture' in Dutt's terms – are unaffected by institutional forms of inequality based on class, caste or ethnicity. This made the 'folk' non-contemporaneous with modern India. However, the tension between the universal and the local that informs the work of both Coomaraswamy and Dutt has been extremely productive for folklore scholarship, as we shall see in the next section.

LOCAL CULTURE AND PAN-INDIAN CIVILIZATION

It is important to remember that in Coomaraswamy's scheme the local has a place within the universal. Regional culture is subsumed within pan-Indian civilization. For him, the category of folk is a way of producing the local (cf. Appadurai 1997) that must in turn address the universal. This idea has been used by some Bengali folklorists to re-constitute Bengal's regional culture. Thus as I have discussed earlier, Roychaudhury (1996) finds in Purulia *chhó* the living memory of a classical dance tradition that has vanished from the urban areas. Interestingly Roychaudhury's work combines aspects of the two perspectives discussed above. She follows Coomaraswamy in thinking that there has been an interchange between folk and aristocratic (she calls this classical) forms of culture over time. But she also shares with Dutt the opinion that Bengal has a distinctive regional culture that is threatened by the presence of an outward oriented elite. Unlike Dutt, however, she locates this elite not in the medieval period but in the colonial period of Bengal's history.[10] Roychaudhury tries to reconstitute a Bengali aesthetic within the perspective of pan-Indian civilization.[11]

Other scholars speaking from the vantage point of tribal studies say that some groups whom they characterise as *jana*, that is egalitarian tribal societies, are qualitatively different from the rest of India, which is dominated by institutionalised systems of inequality based on caste (*jāti*) (Bosu Mullick 1991). Arguing against the official representation of Indian culture as a 'unity in diversity', Bosu Mullick says that this was "the diversity of incompatible qualities. And its unity was not the unity of agreeable diversities"(1991:vi). He says that historically, mainstream Indian society dominated by caste ideology has always rejected the tribal groups (*jana societies*) that lived in their midst. Bosu Mullick is speaking specifically about the tribal groups who inhabit the Chota Nagpur plateau in Central India. Many of the tribal groups in this region have a history of rebellion against the colonial administration in the past and more recently against the Indian state. According to Bosu Mullick, the movement for the separate tribal state and the assertion of a collective tribal identity has reaffirmed the common values between the different groups as well as intensifying their sense of separation from mainstream caste society. Bosu Mullick's views on regional distinctiveness resonate with those of Gurusaday Dutt. It is important to note, however, that he is the only scholar discussed so far who speaks of caste inequality. But this is achieved only by separating the 'folk' into tribal and peasant societies. (The latter being seen as part of an essentially stratified social formation.) Another point worth noting is that he includes Purulia in the Chota Nagpur cultural region that he calls the society of *janas* or tribes. Mahua Roychaudhury, whose views have been presented above, includes the folk dances of Purulia within the culture of Bengal and would like to see them reconstituted as classical or *margic* forms based on the canonical Indian text, the *Natyashastra.*[12] To understand Purulia's dual identity- as part of the tribal culture of Chota Nagpur as well as the folk culture of Bengal we have to first determine the political stakes involved in such classification. After independence, the Indian state invested considerable resources in the revival of Indian aesthetic traditions. This meant that regional forms were often recast as 'classical' traditions, which were thought to reflect the cultural unity of the country (or rather its 'unity in diversity'). At the same time as this was happening, India was also being reorganised into states on the basis of common language. Overtime this has led to the growth of a regional chauvinism and to competition between regions for cultural recognition by the government (Swapnasundari 2005). Both Roychaudhury and Bosu Mullick are speaking about the production of locality as Appadurai says but within a global context. For Bosu Mullick this global context is a syncretic tribal society that has always co-existed uneasily with the rest of India and for Roychaudhury it is a syncretic Bengali culture that must find its distinctive voice within Indian civilization.

SECULARISM AND THE FOLK

Since the early part of the twentieth century nationalist Bengali folklorists have characterised the voice of the Bengali folk as intrinsically secular (Sarkar 1941, Sen 1985). At first sight this seems to contradict Coomaraswamy's view of folk culture as essentially sacred. Is it still possible to speak of a nationalist discourse in the face of such divergent views? For the early Bengali folklorists, the portrayal of the folk as secular was a strategic devise by which they were able to establish Bengal's distinctiveness without repudiating her place within the civilizational mainstream. Under the influence of orientalist representations of Indian civilization, scholars like Coomaraswamy tended to underplay the significance of the Muslim period and characterised Indian civilization as essentially Hindu. Bengal was home to a large Muslim population and had many heterodox sects and cults that bore the traces of ancient Buddhist and pre-Aryan practices. By characterising Bengali culture as folk culture and emphasizing its syncretic nature the Bengali nationalists were able to locate Bengal's culture within the dominant civilizational paradigm. Hindus and Muslims were thought to share a common culture that was secular and worldly. The gods and goddesses glorified in popular religious rituals shared by both religious communities were human figures expressing human interests. Thus folk culture was essentially universal and the folk in all parts of the country and at all times, shared the same concerns. Secularism was presented as a primordial sentiment of the folk.[13] In more recent times it is used by Left oriented intellectuals to counter the cultural nationalism propagated by right-wing political parties. Thus suggesting that secularism is an indigenous value. In this context women become the privileged representatives of folk culture – the subaltern voice that cuts across such conflicting divisions such as those based on class, caste, religion and locality (Sinha 1997).

In this essay we get a somewhat different representation of the 'folk' than the common sense connotation of the term. The 'folk' suggests a bounded community in which face-to-face relations predominate. In contrast to 'civilization' that connotes universalism, 'folk' connotes localisation (Chatterji 2003). Coomaraswamy (1956), as we saw, thinks of folklore as a civilizational category. Even Dutt (1990) who has a more conventional understanding of the concept of folk does however think that it has an important role in the revitalisation of national culture, which has to be built up through dialogue between different regional traditions. Why is folklore so often used to reconstitute national culture especially in newly emerging nations? The 'folk' is a complex semic category suggesting both a primordial sentiment as well as contemporary orientation such that it can refer to tradition as well as co-exist with modern social formations. Let me explain what I mean by citing an example from a different region and from another folk genre – the folk painting of Mithila in Bihar. Santosh Kumar Das, an artist trained in modern art techniques, has returned to the traditional folk style of his community to depict a contemporary event – the communal riots in Gujarat in 2002. In a sensitive analysis of the paintings, Mani Shekhar Singh (2007) explores the artist's consciousness, the reasons he may have had for choosing to return to a style that he had earlier repudiated. As Singh says, "the Gujarat series is a lament, an expression of a sense of loss of tradition articulated by the artist in the face of painful change initiated by *Hindutva*[14] politics. As the compositions in the series make evident, not only humans but also Hindu gods and goddesses mourn this loss and destruction... By making the gods into witnesses as well as party to his lamentation, Santosh transforms the Gujarat riots of 2002 from a local tragedy into a catastrophic event of cosmic proportion" (ibid.: 10-11). It is the unique capacity of folk culture to address the universal from its vantage point in the local that makes it an indispensable part of contemporary Indian society.

Can the category of 'tribe' take the universalistic orientation that folk culture is made to adopt in the writings of the nationalist folklorists? As we saw in the chapters on Bhadu and the *jhūmūr*, attempts to transpose models of folk culture built on Hindu-Muslim peasant interaction onto tribal-Hindu relations have led to contradictions in the way that society in Purulia is perceived. However recent writings by activist scholars from Purulia and Jharkhand do strive for an interpretation of tribal culture that is global and universalistic in orientation. This was brought home to me on the occasion of the *Baha* festival celebrated at the Indira Gandhi National Centre of the Arts (IGNCA), New Delhi on the 23rd of April, 2006. The choice of the *Baha* festival that is celebrated by many different tribal groups in the Jharkhand region under different names, signalled this new orientation. The ritual worship in the morning – creating a *sarna* (sacred grove) in the manicured lawns of the IGNCA was a way of marking it out as a privileged site – making it the site of 'a cosmic invitation to the earth', to quote from B.K. Roy Burman's speech on the occasion, which is what *Baha* is. The conference that followed offered philosophical reflection on tribal religion. Individual speakers spoke about the symbolism of the ritual and on the 'tribalness' as a way of being, as an orientation to life, nature and society. What all the speakers stressed was not the distinctiveness of specific tribal ways of life, nor plurality or diversity but rather global values that natural religion can offer to other faiths; values such as environmental protection, reciprocity with nature and the world, self-restraint and sociality which are embodied in the *Baha* festival of flowers and vegetation. All the presentations stressed the fact that tribal cultures represent the ancient, the beginning of human civilization, the traces of what is left after repeated conquests which began in the sub-continent, perhaps, with the coming of the Aryans. *Adi Dharam* represents the womb from which all religions and civilizations emerge. It is not possible to talk of tribal culture as a distinctive stream within Indian civilization. As Kalyan Kumar Chakravarti said, "We were all tribal once. Some of us have been de-tribalised."

This mode of interpreting tribal culture emerges from a specific historical context and discourse in nineteenth century Chota Nagpur – that of the Christian missionary writings on tribal theology. I give a brief account of their writings as a way of contrasting two genres of scholarship on tribal culture from contiguous areas – Purulia and Jharkhand.

Christianity according to these missionary scholars shares a common ethos with tribal religion. The specific features shared by both religions are the idea of revelation within the context of a natural and organic community, the idea of an original fall that is responsible for the human condition of the world, and the idea of a transcendental and divine spirit. Thus Minz (1997) says that the tribal religion of Chota Nagpur expresses the organic interrelatedness of god, man, nature and spirit. The tribal way of life expresses this interconnectedness and like the ideal Christian believer the tribal person exists for the sake of others. These others take the form of ancestors, the tribal community, truth and god (van den Bogaert 1993). Just as the church is the expression of the authentic Christian community so also is the tribal *panchāyat* the seat of collective decision making and the locus of truth telling the embodiment of authentic tribal community (van den Bogaert 1993). From this perspective then the conversion of tribal people to Christianity does not lead to the destruction of tribal religion but rather to its renewal.[15] The tribal belief system of Chota Nagpur comes to stand for the religion of the Old Testament. Therefore just as the New Testament completes the message of the Old Testament so also will Christianity complement and develop the spiritual message of tribal religion (Minz 1997, Kerketta 1987). However, for tribal religion to be related analogically to the Old Testament religion both this religion as well as Christianity have to be reconfigured. This is done through a series of displacements that effectively reconstitute both the collective identities of particular groups in this region as well as the histories of particular religious orders and the politics of religious conversion. The tribal Christian church is supposed to be similar to the original church of the Gospels and very different from the Western individualistic and atomistic world view that is often Christian in name only (Minz 1997). The process by which an ideal tribal identity is constituted by excluding some tribal groups will be discussed in the next section. Here I will confine myself to stating that there are many tribal groups in Chota Nagpur with diverse customs and beliefs. Therefore, 'the tribal way of life' described by these scholars is an ideal type abstracted from the life styles of particular tribal groups. Tribal society is supposed to be fundamentally egalitarian and to have resisted incorporation within both caste and feudal society. Not only does this perspective deny the influence of Hinduism and Islam both of which have had a historical presence in this region but it also excludes groups that share common customs and beliefs with so called tribal groups that have participated in the process of state formation and who see themselves as sharing both a kshatriya as well as tribal identity (Sinha 1995, Beiteille 1986).

THE PRIMORDIAL VERSUS THE SUPERNATURAL

Unlike many anthropological representations of folk religion the representation of these tribal missionary scholars is constituted through myth rather than ritual.[16] For them myths embody doctrine and to the extent that tribal religion has an autonomous identity it must have a doctrinal base. This is achieved by privileging a certain set of origin myths such that tribal religion can be constituted as an organised system of beliefs and practices that are in accord with a particular cosmological ordering. This allows beliefs and practices that are discordant with this ordering to be displaced. I describe the process through which this occurs with reference to one particular tribe in Chota Nagpur – the Munda.

In the way that the Santhals have an iconic status in the writings of Bengali folklorists so also has Munda society a unique position among tribal societies in Chota Nagpur.[17] It has been the focus of scholarly attention since the latter half of the nineteenth century.

Following in the footsteps of the great Jesuit missionaries like Lievens (1856-1893) who established the Roman Catholic church in Chota Nagpur and Hoffman (1857-1928) who compiled the *Encyclopedia Mundarica* (cf. Hoffman and van Emelen 1965), contemporary Jesuit scholars like van Exem have produced authoritative works on Munda religion. van Exem's, *The Religious System of the Munda Tribe* is considered a land mark in tribal theology (cf. Kerketta 1987), not so much because it argues for a tribal church *per se* but because it sets out the terms by which one particular tribal religion can be compared with Christianity. van Exem (1982), describing his study as an exercise in 'religious anthropology' criticizes anthropologists for too great an emphasis on ritual at the expense of doctrine. This, he says, has led to a skewed portrayal of tribal religion. Instead of the stereotypical representations of tribal religions as being magical and animistic he says that Munda religion is fundamentally monotheistic, non-anthropomorphic and ethical. Even though Munda society lacks scripture its doctrine is found in myth. Munda myths, according to van Exem, are sacred history, for they serve as guidelines for an exemplary life. Not all myths serve this purpose however, and it is the task of the scholar to isolate the key myths that account for the Munda way of life. This van Exem does by examining the myths that are associated with significant rituals, that is, those that describe primordial events. He privileges one particular origin myth that is supposed to account for the Munda's present state of being in terms of a fall from an original state of grace. It also prescribes the customs and rituals that are required to maintain an ethical life within the Munda tribe. This myth, called the Asur legend, has a unique status in Munda mythology, according to van Exem, describing as it does both a primordial event as well as a historical conflict between the ancestors of the Mundas and the Asur tribe who still live in Chota Nagpur today.

The story is as follows: The Asur, a tribe of iron smelters, rebelled against the Supreme Being. They went against the order of creation that he had laid down. They dug the earth and smelted iron all day and all night. The fire from their furnaces laid waste the order of nature on earth and even scorched the heavens, the abode of Sing Bonga, the great god of the Munda tribe. Sing Bonga sent several messengers to the Asur men asking them to restrain their labour, "...If you work the bellows by night, don't do it by day. If you work the bellows by day, don't do it by night. The lotus pond and the marsh flower pool are drying up. The straight-horned heifer and the cow with her curved horns find no water, find no food. Grass and herbs of the earth, trees and shrubs are all withering..." (van Exem 1982: 51). But the Asur, proud of their creative ability did not heed this warning. They set themselves up as demiurges, boasting of their mastery of fire that gave them the ability to reshape nature, to make iron out of ore. Finally Sing Bonga went to the Asur himself disguised as a young boy infected with wounds. The Asur drove him away saying that he was unclean. He took shelter with an old Munda couple, the ancestors of the present Munda. He gave the Asur men several signs of his divinity which they chose to ignore. Finally he tricked them into entering their own furnaces so that they were burnt to death. He transformed the Asur women into spirits and these are the terrestrial *boṇgās* that the Munda tribe still worships.

For van Exem the Asur embody the principle of evil. Thus he gives them a symbolic rather than an empirical status. But this does not mean that history has no place in his interpretation of Munda cosmology. The unique status of the Asur legend given by its dual status as both myth and history allows van Exem to conceptualise Munda religion as an evolving process, shaped by the interaction with belief systems of other tribes. Historically interpreted, the Asur legend becomes an account of how the Munda encounter an alien people and incorporate their spirits into their own cosmology, thus setting the stage for a future interface with another 'alien' religion – Christianity. van Exem's use of both myth and history carries the stamp of Biblical scholarship. History, as in the narratives of both the Old and the New Testament, becomes the arena on which societies relate to God (cf. Daly 1978). The worship of the *boṇgā* spirits, according to this mode of scholarship, can be treated as a historical accretion and therefore possible to excise from the original belief system which according to van Exem and other missionary scholars is fundamentally monotheistic and therefore open to the formation of a tribal church. Unfortunately, even though the conception of a tribal church gives some autonomy to the idea of folk religion it does so by expelling certain tribal groups and their belief systems from the dominant paradigm, thus removing from this representation of folk religion all traces of so called animism. However on the positive side, this representation of tribal religion opens the world to the process of modernisation. For Kerketta (1987), Minz (1997) and others the many tribal movements for religious reform point to the flexibility of tribal religion and its willingness to accept change (cf. Guha 1983, Sarkar 1985). Even though many of these movements failed to achieve their goal, Christianity, these scholars feel, will become the catalyst that will open the tribe to the processes of modernisation not as a passive acceptance that will destroy tribal identity but rather as a new source of identity.

I have discussed van Exem's work at length because it is a forerunner to some new post-modernist literary endeavours that explore the boundaries between oral and literary traditions and ask us to re-think categories such as 'folk' and 'tribe'. Thus Mahashweta Devi (2002), the littérateur and activist for tribal rights, turns to a medieval Bangla epic, the *Vyad Kaand* (Book of the Hunter) of Kavikankan Mukandaram's *Chandi Mangala*, to try and re-construct the lost oral tradition of the Shabar tribe (cf. Chatterji n.d.b;[18] and Nilakanth Ghoshyal turns to the folkloric representations of the Bhadu myth to write *Bhumi Kanya* (Earth Maiden) (see appendix 1). I call these literary endeavours post-modern because they re-contextualise the scholarly folklore discourse as well as the oral traditions that this discourse attempts to thematise (Chatterji 2007a, Warshaver 1991).

As regards the relationship between oral tradition and folk culture, Jawaharlal Handoo (2004), the eminent Indian folklorist has said that we need to reaffirm that relationship as a counter to conventional modes of approaching history and culture that emphasise the 'palace paradigm'. Whilst I agree with Handoo that too much emphasis is placed on dynastic history and less on the structural forms of myth and folklore in popular writings on culture,[19] I would plead for a greater emphasis on the role of princely courts in the development of folk culture especially in border regions where the interface between local and pan-Indian forms is long standing. Hitesh Ranjan Sanyal (2004) is one of the few scholars in India who has considered this interface with some seriousness. Speaking about the border regions of Bengal he says that many of the peripheral principalities were declared to be tributary states owing formal allegiance to the great though distant Moghul Empire.

The geographical distance between the central authority and these border states gave the latter some amount of autonomy. Thus they were able to selectively adopt elements of Moghul culture while retaining much of what was traditionally available. The Moghul presence was thought to be alien but distant enough to be non-threatening, and local courts could use Moghul models as sites for experimentation. Traces of this self-conscious adoption of high culture aspects is, according to Sanyal, still visible in the peasant societies of these border regions. Thus many genres of 'folk' song in Bengal have cultivated and popular forms that require different performative contexts from the ones conventionally associated with folk performances. It can be argued that princely courts no longer exist in independent India and contexts in which institutions such as the *nāchnī nāch* first developed are no longer available for study. However it is important to give historical depth to folklore wherever possible, especially at a time of rapid social change. It is sometimes said that it is only with the development of writing that self-consciousness develops in cultures. This may not always be the case as we see in the case of these border principalities where cultivated and 'folk' variants of songs that belong to the same genre co-exist in collective memory. It is not as if writing played no part in the transmission of cultural forms in these societies. It did not suppress oral transmission and in fact even enhanced orality (Kirshenblatt-Gimblet 1998). According to Kirshenblatt-Gimblet (1998) 'inscription' creates a gap between words and speakers, a space that allows for creative innovation. The history of medieval Bangla literature shows evidence of this fact. Scholars like Sukumar Sen (1960) and Dinesh Chandra Sen (1986) have shown how literary texts such as the *mangala kāvyas* in the seventeenth and eighteenth centuries evolved from myths and sacred stories that were part of the oral tradition. We see another period of innovation in folk culture that is being driven by inscription – that is the present. Literary works and folklore scholarship as I have shown are providing an impetus for change in folk culture. It is important for folklorists to reflect on the impact that their writings have made on folk culture, on the process of change but also on their contribution in sustaining folk forms as living traditions.

NOTES

1. In fact, in his *History of Bengali Language and Literature*, Sen (1986) recounts that Sir Ashutosh Mukherjee, the vice chancellor of Calcutta University in the first decade of the 20th century, had asked him to collect 'folk literature' so that a case could be made for starting a Bengali literature department in the university. Sen says that he was asked to demonstrate that Bengal did have a literature of sufficient antiquity for it to become a university discipline. It is interesting that the folk are used to give historical depth to Bengali culture.
2. Gurusaday Dutt started the *Bratachari* movement in the 1930s, with the goal of developing the physical and moral faculties of the youth through the medium of folk culture (Sen Gupta 1965). Influenced by Baden-Powell's Boy Scouts movement and impressed by the revival of folk dances and songs in England that he witnessed when he visited England in 1929, he felt that the 'discipline' and 'spirit of cooperation' that had once characterised the 'races' of Bengal could still be found in the dances of the folk groups.
3. Reviews of plays like *Riot* that has thematised the *chhó* as part of its plot structure and the serialisation of the novel *Bhumi Kanya* by Nilkantha Ghoshyal, which humanises the Bhadu story, in the popular literary magazine *Desh* testify to this (see appendix 1).
4. The plan was to separate Bihar, Orissa and a large part of east Bengal which had a predominantly Muslim population and conjoin it with Assam.
5. Rabindranath Tagore was one of the first collectors of folk rhymes in Bangla and he published two such collections in 1884 and 1895. Another important collection was published in 1899 by Jogindranath Sarkar. Dinesh Chandra Sen, a protégé of Tagore, is considered to be one of the foremost folklorists of Bengal. He was appointed a research fellow by Sir Ashutosh Mukherji, and given funds to collect and document oral stories from the Ramayana in the 1910s and 20s. Tagore's nephew, Abanindranath Tagore and Aghorenath Chattopadhya, published collections of stories narrated during domestic rituals in 1919 and 1897 respectively. Dakshinaranjan Mitra Mazumdar's collection of folk tales, first published in 1907, soon became famous. It was included in the anthropology syllabus of Calcutta University and was translated into German in 1919. Many of these collectors were members of the *Bangiya Sahitya Parishad* (Bengal Literary Association) that sponsored the publication of nationalist literature (Haque 1976).
6. However Sarkar (1973) reminds us that the Swadeshi movement tried to use religion (i.e. Hinduism) to reach out to the masses. This inevitably led to the exclusion of Muslims. Folklorists of this period tend to think of Hinduism as an inclusive system of myths and rituals

that incorporates many elements of Buddhism that was a popular religion in Bengal before the twelfth century and of ancient folk and tribal beliefs that were animistic in nature (Sen 1985, Tagore 1919). Sen thought that even though East Bengal had a predominantly Muslim population, Islam was only a superficial veneer. Conversely, B. K. Sarkar (1985) thinks of Islam as a popular religion that drew many followers from Buddhism in Bengal. He says that there is very little difference between Hindu and Muslim peasants as far as religious practices are concerned. They practice a religion that he calls "Bengalicism", an amalgam of ideas and practices that to a large extent precede the coming of both these world religions to Bengal (see also Chatterji n.d.)

7. Though by his own admission, Sudhi Pradhan (1979), one of the members of the Bengal branch of the IPTA feels that the association was more successful with the urban proletariat than with rural peasants.
8. As we shall see Ananda Coomaraswamy and Rabindranath Tagore, especially in his later writings, both held this view. B. K. Sarkar (1985) developed his critique of this representation of Indian society through an examination of folk religion (Chatterji n.d.).
9. In a thought-provoking article on the Crafts' Museum in Delhi, Paul Greenough (1996) describes the linking of a national myth – the existence of a single, unified craft tradition with the unity of India – which is the official ideology of the museum. However, there are often contradictions between practices and ideology within an institution as there are contradictions between the ideologies of different national institutions which Greenough's article fails to capture.
10. To recapitulate Roychaudhury (1996) says that the uncritical admiration of Western culture and the north Indian musical tradition led to the demise of Bengal's distinctive classical dance tradition. The *chhó* is not characterised as a tribal dance in her work for reasons that are obvious.
11. The historian, Hitesh Ranjan Sanyal (2004), believes that the 'region' is the ideal unit for the exploration of the interconnections between *deśī* and *mārgic* aspects of culture. Unlike many anthropologists, (Redfield 1955, Sinha 1957, Marriot 1955), he does not believe that this is an unconscious process. In his study of a small principality in one of the border regions of West Bengal, he shows how the semi-tribal Mulla court in what is now Bardhman district, produced political institutions that self-consciously integrated aspects of the culture of the Mughal court of North India with indigenous elements taken from local tribal and peasant communities. The distance of the Mulla kingdom from North India made the Mughal court seem non-

threatening and allowed it to become a site for experimentation with novelty. Sanyal suggests that folk culture is constituted at three different levels, viz. *jana* (local), *deśa* (regional) and *mārga* (global or pan-Indian). He says that the *deśī* or regional level acts as a site for mediation between the local and the global.

12. In this regard it is important to remember that the division between folk and classical in also a bureaucratic classification conferred by the Indian state. Dances that are designated as classical have access to the resources of the state (Swapanasundari 2005).
13. See also Asad (2002).
14. This refers to the political activity of right-wing fundamentalist parties in India.
15. Tribal conversions to Hinduism make the same argument though the points of contact between the two religions is usually thought to be animism or natural religion with which folk Hinduism has a deep affinity.
16. According to Sontheimer (1995) both folk and tribal religions are 'ways of doing' rather than 'ways of saying'.
    Many of these missionary scholars are *ādivāsīs* themselves, while others like van Exem have the honorary status of *ādivāsī* conferred upon them.
17. The location of Rabindranath Tagore's institution, Vishwa Bharati in Birbhum, a Santhal dominated area and Tagore's preeminence among literature and folklore scholars have given Santhal society an archetypal status as the ideal tribal society as we saw in the chapter on the *jhūmūr*.
18. As a former 'criminal' tribe, the stigmatised Shabar have lost their sense of collective history and mythic consciousness, according to Mahashweta Devi (2002).
    The 'Criminal Tribes'Act' was passed in 1871 by the British Indian Government. It was believed that certain groups within the caste system were 'criminals' by hereditary occupation. Meena Radhakrishna (2001) says that this act was based on assumptions about 'vagrancy' and impoverishment that was associated with forms of life that were considered nomadic. Such groups were forced to adopt a sedentary way of life. After independence such groups were re-designated as de-notified tribes.
19. We saw evidence of the distortions that too great an emphasis on dynastic history can have on myth in the chapter on Bhadu where scholars have assumed that the myth can be read as a historical account.

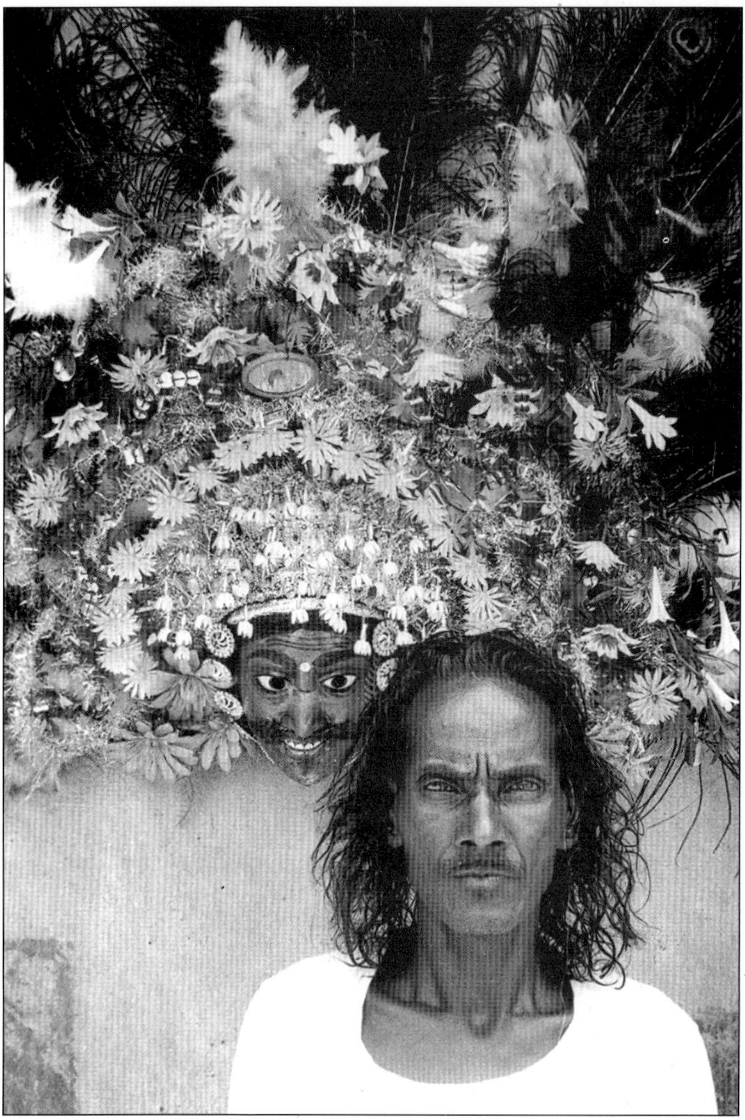

Gambhir Singh Mura with a *kirāta* mask.

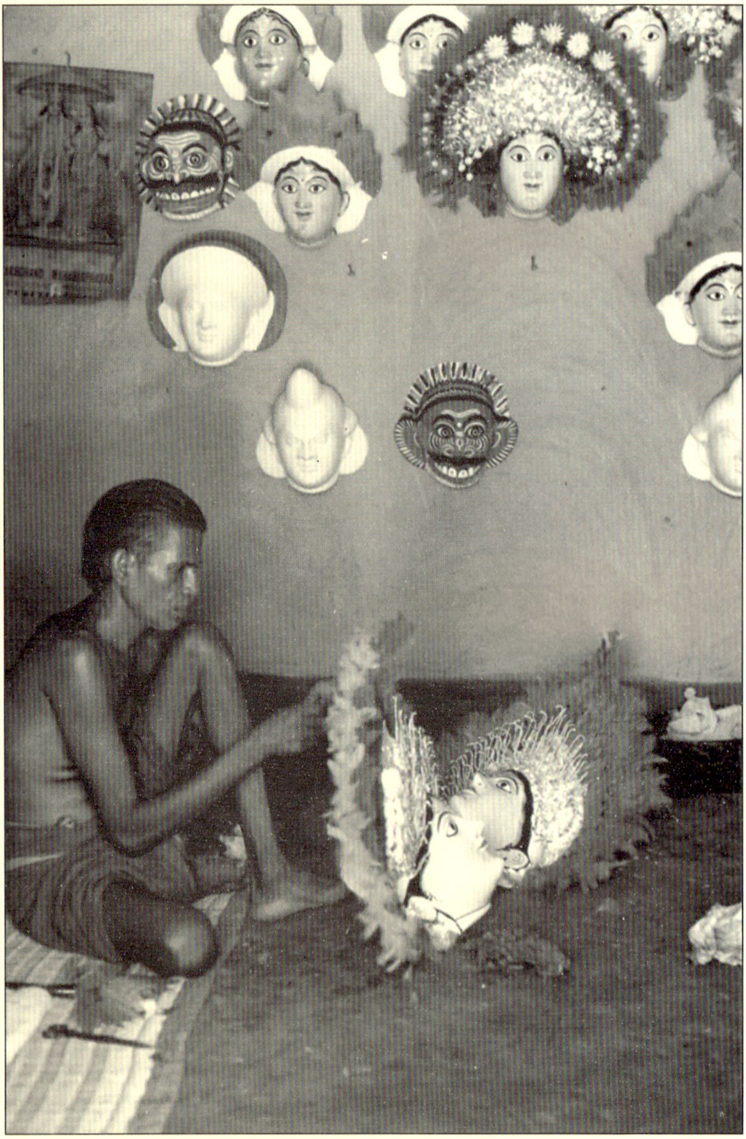

A Shutradhar man putting the finishing touches to a dance mask.

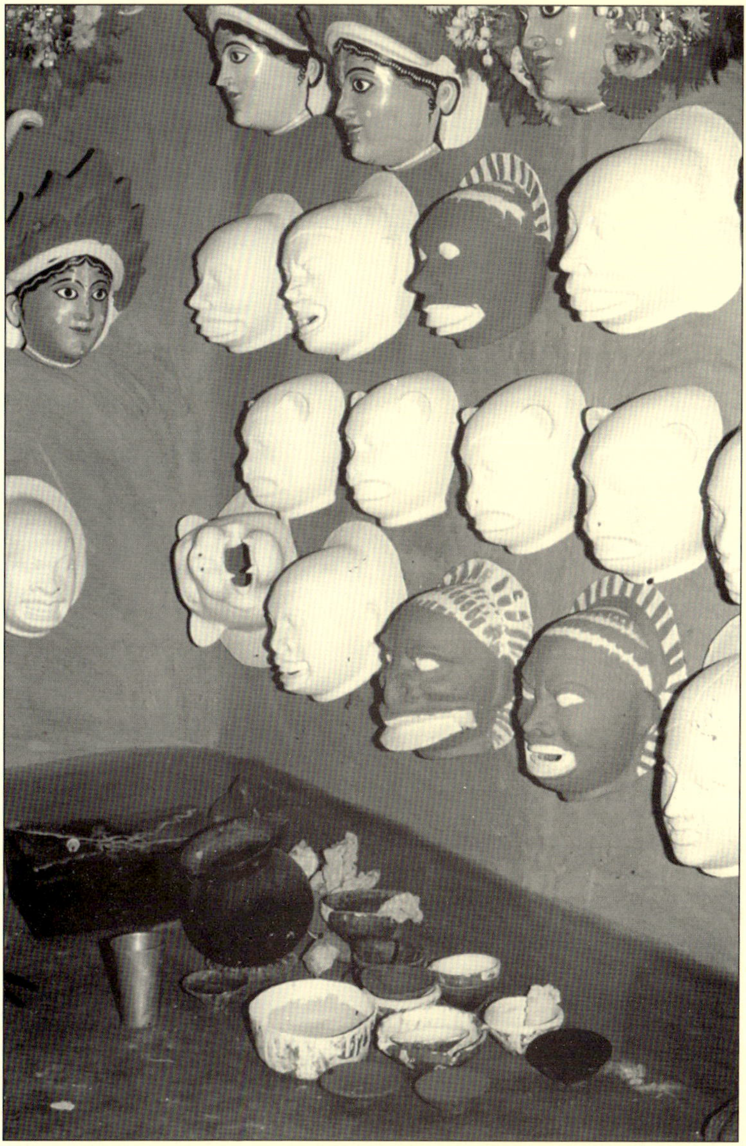

A mask makers *karkhana*.

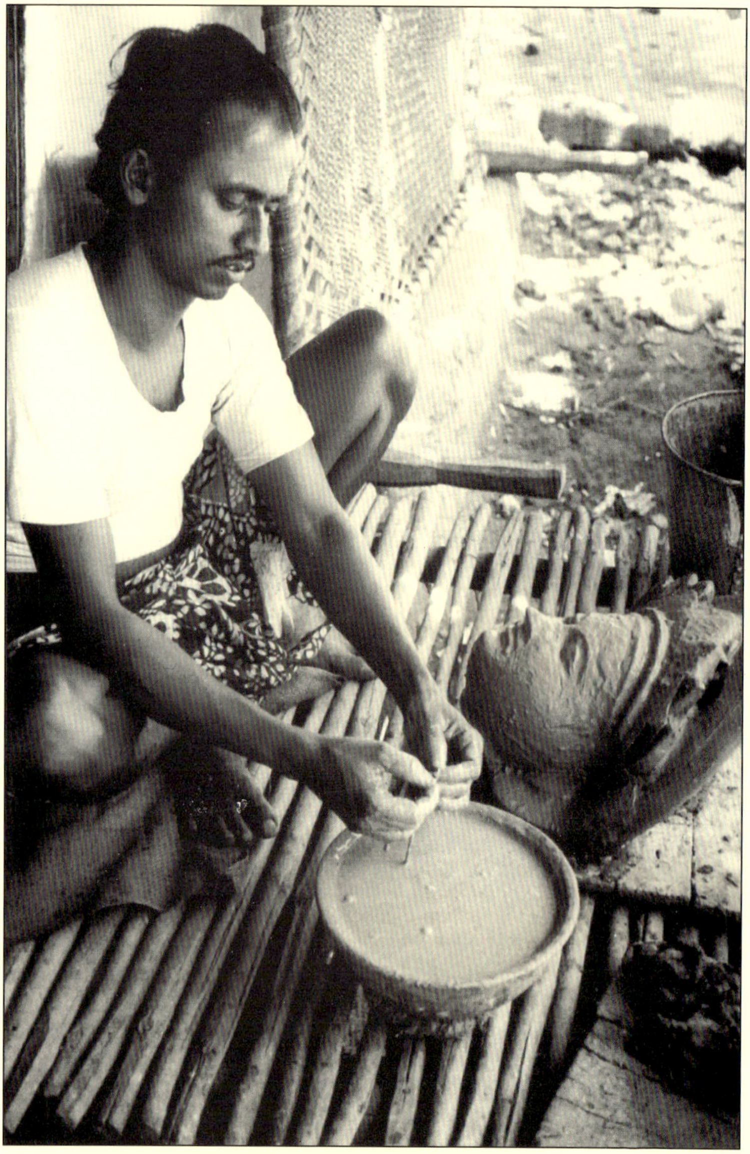

A Shutradhar man making the mould for a dance mask.

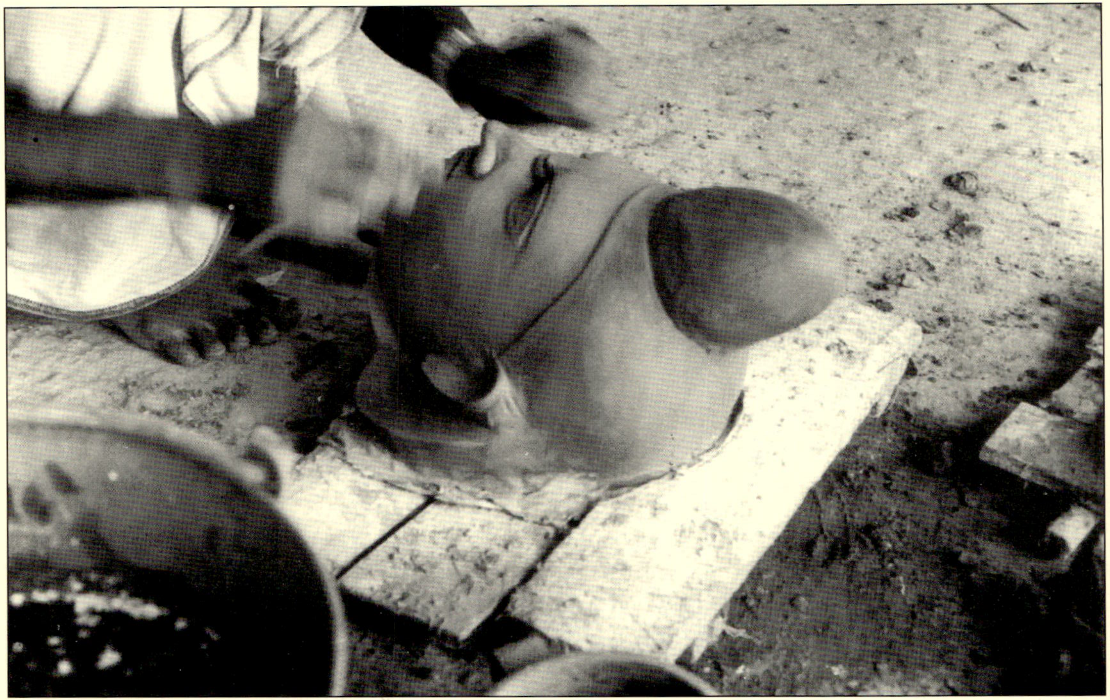

The mould of a Shiva mask.

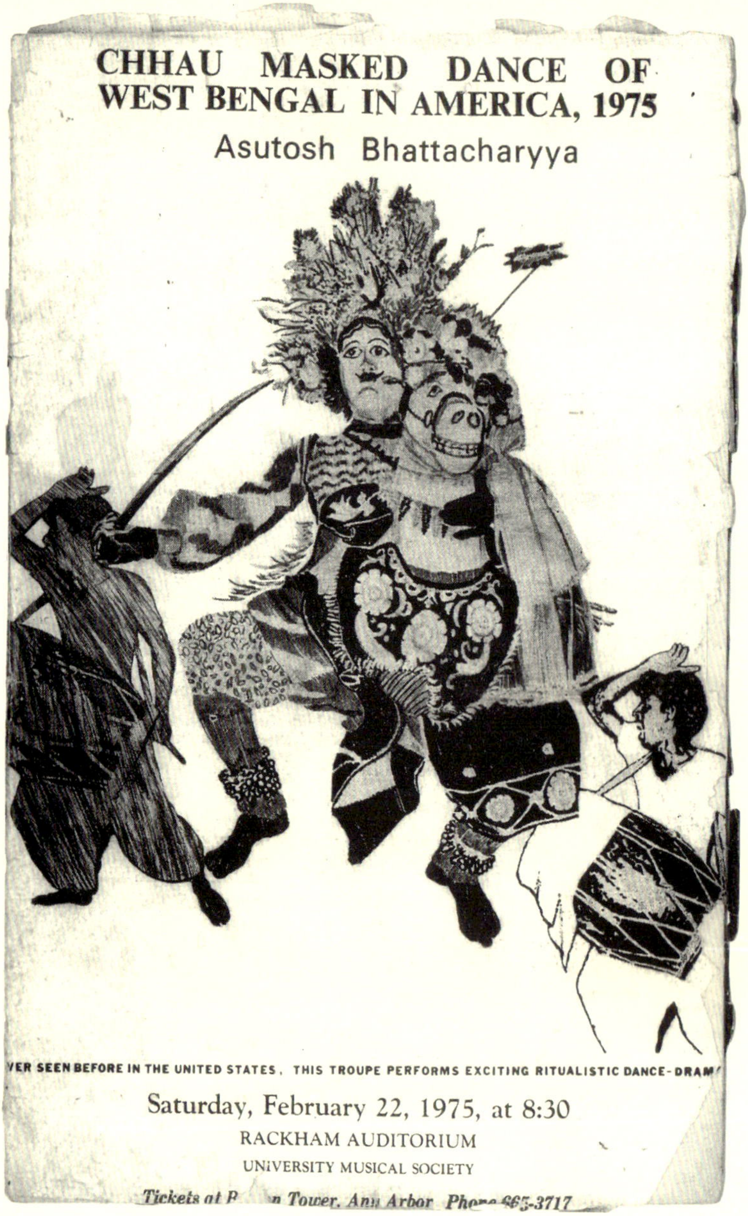

Dance programme printed on the occasion of the Chorida dance troupe's first tour of the USA.

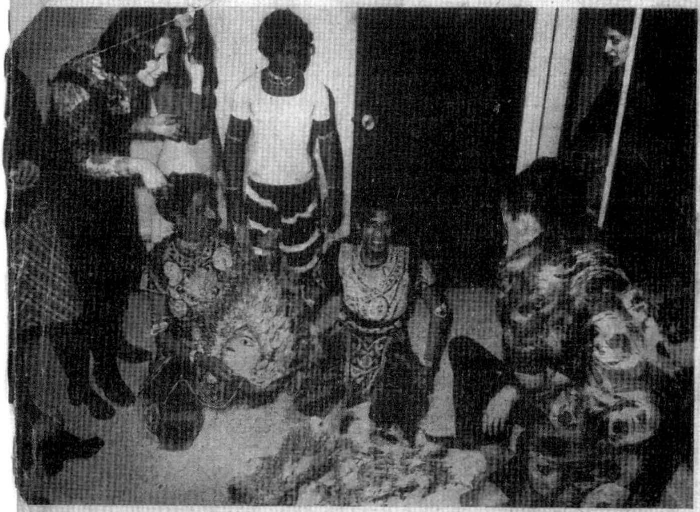

American women examining some masks at the back stage of Carnegie Hall. New York.

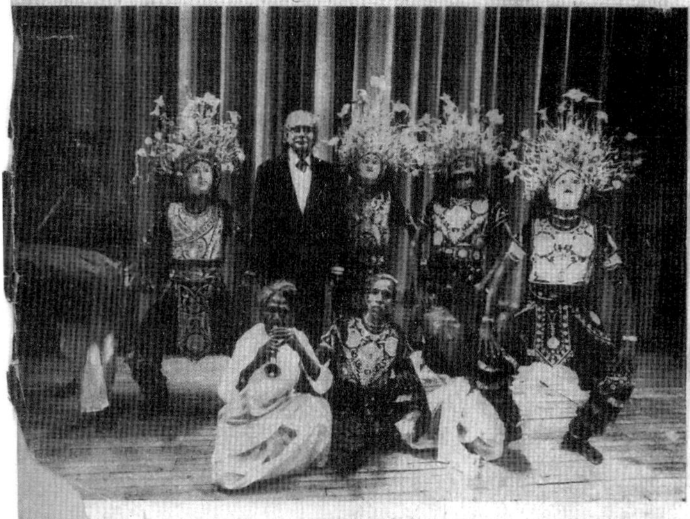

:haryya with some artistes at the Carnegie Hall Stage, New York

Back cover of the same programme. The two pictures depict some famous dancers and include a rare photography of Ashutosh Bhattacharya.

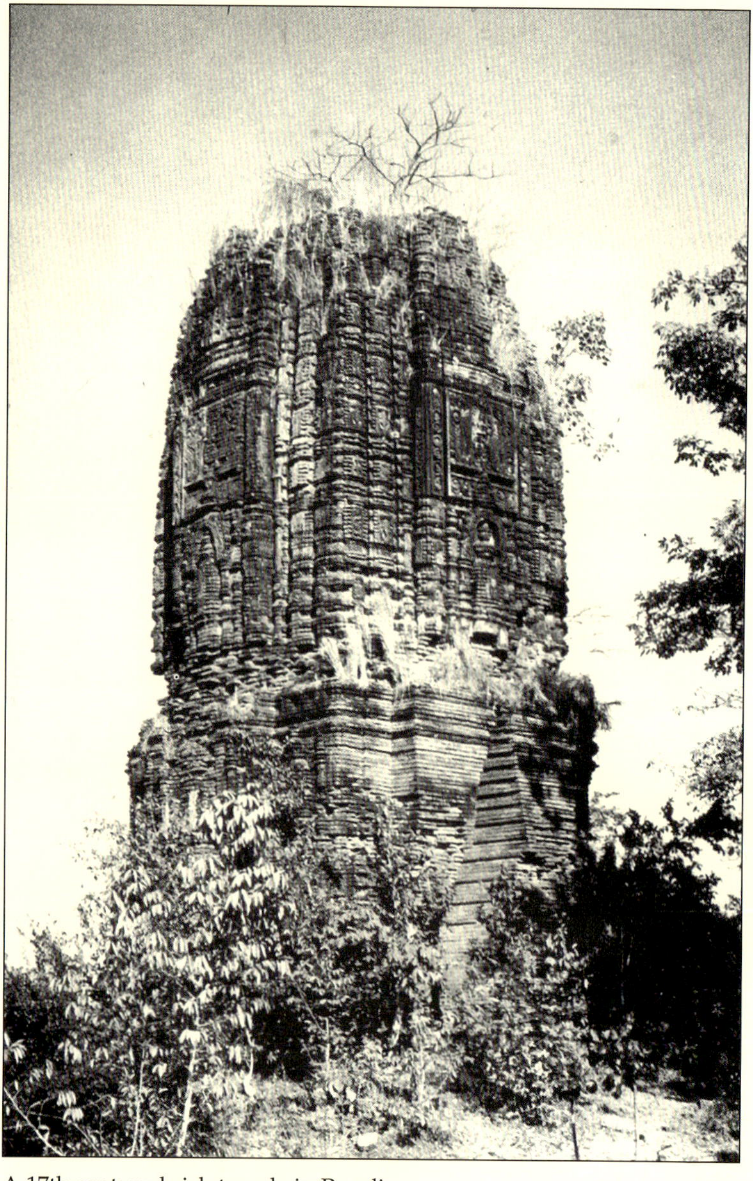

A 17th century brick temple in Purulia.

Appendix One

The Story of *Bhumi Kanya* (Earth Maiden) by Nilakantha Ghoshyal. (Serialised in *Desh Patrika* between December 2004 and April 2005)

Folklorist Papiya is researching Bhadu *pūjā* in Purulia when she comes across Herambh Bauri (a low caste man) who tells her the secret story of Bhadu's life. Bhadu was an orphan found by the chief (*mukhya*) of Lada village. Raja Nilmoni Singh of Kashipur in whose kingdom Ladha is located has just introduced a new strain of paddy –Bhaduyi – for cultivation in Kashipur. He tours the kingdom, disguised as an alien traveller, to see if his subjects are in favour of the new crop. He is accompanied by his minister Dhruvachand. In the course of their travels they hear that the chief of Lada village has a daughter who is the living embodiment of Lakshmi, the goddess of prosperity. He decides to see her in person and visits Lada disguised as a Sanskrit *pundit* (scholar). He is wonderstruck at her beauty and grace and decides to adopt her as his daughter. However since her father, the village chief, will not let her go away, he decides to let Bhadu stay in the village but to be educated in a manner befitting a royal princess. Dhruvachand stays behind to oversee her education. Bhadu's new identity – as a royal princess is kept secret. Bhadu is very popular among the village people as she works actively for their betterment. It is while providing succor to the villagers during an epidemic that she meets Anjan the son of a doctor (*kavirāj*) of a neighbouring village. They fall in love much to the dismay of

Dhruvachand. In the meantime the king is imprisoned because of his active involvement in the 1857 uprising. He is later released. When he hears about Bhadu's involvement with Anjan, he orders the latter's capture and imprisonment. Bhadu is heartbroken and accompanied by two friends she travels across the kingdom singing songs at the gates of all the forts where Anjan may possibly be imprisoned, hoping that he will recognise her voice and respond. The king finally has a change of heart and releases Anjan, but by then Bhadu has disappeared. Her companions report that one morning she seemed to fade away, merging with the sky. Village women continue to sing the songs that Bhadu first sand in the fruitless search for her lover.

(As will be evident some of the details of the story have been taken from folklore writings on Bhadu. In fact, positioning Papiya, the main addressee in the frame narrative in the text, as a researcher signals the novel's self-conscious location vis-à-vis the larger discourse of folklore. Bhadu is also the subject of a recent play that was performed in Calcutta. Interestingly in the play she is portrayed as a Santhal goddess [*Telegraph*, Calcutta, June 17, 2000]).

Appendix Two

Jotil Rai, a school teacher in Chorida village where I did fieldwork in the eighties, composed these two *jhūmūr* songs on the theme of the Great Famine of 1943. Jotil Rai belonged to one of the prominent Bhatt (genealogist) families in Chorida. He was no longer alive when I lived in the village. These two songs were given to me by his widow.

Bhādóró āshīnó bauṛóyī ṭānéró d̄īn
Khūṇjīlé nāhī mīlé rīn
Kīśé dūṭī kāṭōbó d̄īn
Āgé geló ghóṭī thālā
Taubé geló hāthér bālā
Pauré dekhābek bīdhóbārī chīn
Pāmóró Jóṭīló
Jómī bāṭī shaub khoiló
Jīyóntó maurāró ódhīn
Kīśé dūṭī kāṭóbó d̄īn

Bhadro and Ashwin are times of great strain
Even by searching one cannot get loans
How will I pass my days
First went the pots and dishes
Then went the bangles
(from my wife's arms)
Now she wears the symbols of widowhood

(jewellery on a married woman is auspicious)
Jotil mourns
Land and house went
Living is enslaved by death
How will I live out my days

Saun teró śó paunchāś śāl
Āśīné bhīśón ākāl gó
Ei kāl būjhī kāl śaumó hóló
Kī bólī bhāi śaubé bóndhū bólī
Déśé kī haubé kī hóló
Baudón bhóré śaubé mīlé śaubé hórī hórī bauló
Ṭākā chaul ek pāi tāu śomāe mīlé nāi
Kī bhābé prān bañché bauló
Tāi bólī bóndhū śaubé hórī hórī bauló
Jinnī hólén kóṭādār
Mūchḥ chāhā tār bebóhār
Dhaurmā dhórmī śaukólé tejīló
Tāi bólī bóndhū śaubé hórī hórī bauló
Déśé kī haubé kī hóló

The year 1350 (Bengali shaka)
(There is) a great famine in the month of Ashwin (September–October)
With this famine it seems that time has come to an end
I say to my brothers and friends all
What will happen to the country, what has happened
Full-throated let us all chant "Hari, Hari" together
Rice that is worth one pai now sells for a rupee and even that is not always available
How will we keep our souls alive
Therefore I say friends all chant "Hari, Hari"
The keeper of the rations is whimsical – he behaves differently with different people
All have sacrificed *dharma*
Therefore I say friends all chant "Hari, Hari" together
What will happen in the country, what has happened

The terrible famine of 1943 (BS 1350) is called the *bón jhāṛā ākāl* (forest winnowing famine) in Purulia. According to collective memory every last 'edible' root and leaf was gathered and even the husk of the paddy grains was boiled and eaten – such was the severity of the hunger. The famine caused major structural dislocation in Chorida and members of practically every household could recount tales of the menfolk in their family that had left the village to go to Assam to work in the tea plantations – selling themselves as bonded labour. Some of the more enterprising Shutradhar men (caste of carpenters and image makers) made wooden dolls and walked all the way to Assam to try and sell them.

Jotil Rai's widow also gave me the following song about the 'coolies' who went to Assam:

Ḍāl bhāt romā sījā
Khāeñ ré lé món
Ār kulhī chólīló ré jaunómér mótón
Rél chāpīé kulhīr ānódītó món
Ār kūlhī chólīló jaunómér mótón

Lentils, rice and boiled gram
Eat for the last time to your hearts content
And the coolie goes for the rest of his life
Riding in the train (for the first time) the coolie's heart is happy
And the coolie goes for the rest of his life

Bibliography

Anderson, Benedict, 1983. *Imagined Communities.* London: Verso.

Appadurai, Arjun, 1997. *Modernity at Large. Cultural Dimensions of Globalization.* New Delhi: Oxford University Press.

Asad, Talal, 2002. *Formations of the Secular.* Stanford: Stanford University Press.

Ashley, Wayne, 1993. *Recording Ritual. Theatre and Political Display in Kerala State, South India.* (Ph.D. thesis, New York University).

Bakhtin, Michael, 1986. *Speech Genres and Other Late Essays.* Austin: Texas University Press.

Banerjee, Sumanta, 1989. *The Parlour and the Streets. Elites and Popular Culture in Nineteenth Century Calcutta.* Calcutta: Seagull Books.

——, 2002. *Logic in a Popular Form. Essays on Popular Religion in Bengal.* Calcutta: Seagull Books.

Bannerji, Himani, 1998. *The Mirror of Class. Essays on Bengali Theatre.* Calcutta: Papyrus.

Barthes, Roland, 1967. *Elements of Semiology.* New York: Hill and Wang.

——, 1990. "The Grain of the Voice", in S. Firth and A. Goodwin (eds.), *On Record: Rock, Pop and the Written Word.* London: Routledge (51-110).

Beane, Wendell Charles, 2001. *Myth, Cult and Symbols in Shakta Hinduism: A Study of the Indian Mother Goddess.* New Delhi: Munshiram Manoharlal.

Beiteille, Andre, 1986. "The Concept of Tribe with Special Reference to India", *European Journal of Sociology* 27 (297-318).

Bhaba, Homi, 1994. *The Location of Culture.* New York: Routledge.

Bhattacharya, Ashutosh, 1962. *Bangla Loksahitya.* Vol. I. Calcutta: Calcutta Book House.

——, 1965. *BanglarLoksahitya.* Vol. III. Calcutta: Calcutta Book House.
——, 1975. *Chhau: Masked Dances of West Bengal in America.* Calcutta: Research Institute of Folk Culture.
Bhattacharyya, Narendra Nath, 1973. *History of the Shakta Religion.* New Delhi: Munshiram Manoharlal.
Bhattacharya, Rimli, 2002. "The Nautee in the Second City of the Empire." Unpublished paper.
Bhattacharya, Tarundev, 1986. *Purulia.* Calcutta: Firma KLM Pvt. Ltd.
Blackburn, Stuart, 2003. *Print, Folklore and Nationalism in Colonial India.* Delhi: Permanent Black.
Bose, Nirmal Kumar, 1975. *The Structure of Hindu Society.* Delhi: Orient Longman.
Bosu Mullick, S. (ed.), 1991. *Cultural Chotanagpur: Unity in Diversity.* Delhi: Uppal Publishing House.
Briggs, Charles L., 1993. "Metadiscursive Practices and Scholarly Authority in Folkloistics", *The Journal of American Folklore.* Vol. 106, No. 422 (387-434).
Cantlie, Audrey, 2003. "Myth, Text and Context", in Veena Das (ed.), *The Oxford India Companion to Sociology and Social Anthropology.* Delhi: Oxford University Press (827-860).
Castoriadis, Cornelius, 1987. *The Imaginary Institution of Society.* Cambridge: MIT Press.
Chakraborty, Sudhir, 1966 (1397 B.S.), *Bangla Gaaner Shondhane.* Calcutta: Aruna Prokashini.
Chakravarti, Nitish, 2001. *Nachni: The Dancing Girls of Rural Bengal.* Hoogly: Saptarshi Prakashan.
Chakravarti, Subrata, 2001. *Bhadu.* Calcutta: Loksanskriti and Adivasi Sanskriti Kendra.
Chatterjee, Partha, 1993. *The Nation and its Fragments.* Delhi: Oxford University Press.
Chatterji, Roma, 1987. *Folklore and the Formation of Popular Consciousness in a Village in the Purulia District of West Bengal.* (Ph.D. thesis, University of Delhi).
——, 1995. "Authenticity and Tradition. Reappraising a 'Folk' Form", in Vasudha Dalmia and Henri von Stietencron (eds.), *Representing Hinduism: The Construction of Religious Tradition and National Identity.* New Delhi: Sage (420-44).
——, 1998. "Laughter and Dissent: Celebratory Laughter and Collective Life", *Update Quarterly* 4 (10-14).
——, 2002. "Masculine Genres and Feminine Voices", *Journal of Indian Folkloristics.* Vol. IV, no. (I-16).
——, 2003. "The Category of Folk", in Veena Das (ed.), *The Oxford India Companion to Sociology and Social Anthropology.* Delhi: Oxford University Press (567-597).

——, 2005. "Folklore Genres and the Production of a Cultural Field." Paper presented in the Alan Dundes Lecture Series, Department of Anthropology, University of California at Berkeley.

——, 2007. "The Nationalist Sociology of B.K. Sarkar", in Patricia Uberoi, Nandini Sundar and Satish Deshpande (eds.), *Anthropology in the East. Founders of Indian Sociology and Anthropology.* Delhi: Permanent Black (106-131).

——, 2007a. "Orality, Inscription and the Creation of a New Lore", in *Cultural Analysis* (71-90).

Chattopadhya, Bholanath, 2001. "Manbhumer Jhumur", *Lokshruti.* Vol. 18 (567-597).

Chattopadhya G.P. and A.P. Sinha, 1979. "Akademi of Folklore Ayojeeto Chhonaach Seminar", *Chhatrak.* Vol. III (151-155).

Chattopadhya, Naranarayan, 1999. *Jhumur.* Calcutta: Loksanskriti and Adivasi Sanskriti Kendra.

Coburn, Thomas B., 1988. *Devi Mahatmya: The Crystallization of a Goddess Tradition.* Delhi: Motilal Banarsidass.

Cohen, Anthony P. (ed.), 2000. *Signifying Identities: Anthropological Perspectives on Boundaries and Contested Values.* London: Routledge.

Coomaraswamy, Ananda K., 1956. "The Nature of Folklore and Popular Art", in Ananda K. Coomaraswamy (ed.), *Christian and Oriental Philosophies of Art.* New York: Dover Publications (130-143).

Daly, Robert J. (S.J.), 1978. *Christian Sacrifice: The Judeo-Christian Background Before Origin.* Washington D.C.: The Catholic University of America Press.

Das, Veena, 1998. "Narrativizing the Male and Female in Tulasidas' Ramacharitamanasa", in A.M. Shah, B.S. Baviskar and E.A. Ramaswamy (eds.), *Social Structure and Change.* Vol. V. *Religion and Kinship.* Delhi: Sage (46-66).

——, 2006. *Life and Words Violence and the Descent into the Ordinary.* Delhi: Oxford University Press.

Deleuze, Giles, 1991. *Bergsonism.* New York: Zone Books.

Devi, Mahashweta, 2002. *The Book of the Hunter* (trans. from Bangla by Sagaree and Mandira Sengupta). Calcutta: Seagull.

Dutt, Gurusaday, 1954. *The Folk Dances of Bengal.* Calcutta: Estate of Late Sri Gurusaday Dutt.

——, 1990. *Folk Arts and Crafts of Bengal.* Calcutta: Seagull Publications.

Flueckiger, Joyce Burkhalter, 1994. "Genre and Community in the Folklore System of Chattisgarh", in Arjun Appadurai, Frank J. Korom and Margaret Mills (eds.), *Gender, Genre and Power in South Asian Expressive Traditions.* Delhi: Motilal Banarsidass (181-200).

——, 1996. *Gender and Genre in the Folklore of Middle India.* Delhi: Oxford University Press.

Foucault, Michel, 1972. *The Archaeology of Knowledge and the Discourse on Language.* New York: Pantheon Books.

——, 1977. *Language, Counter-Memory, Practice: Selected Essays and Interviews*. Ithaca: Cornell University Press.

Gadamer, Hans-George, 2000. *Truth and Method.* New York: Continuum Press.

Ghosh, Pradeep, 2001. "Prostapona", in Subrata Chakravarti, *Bhadu*. Kolkata: Loksanskriti and Adivasi Sanskriti Kendra (i-ii).

Goodwin, Robert E., 1998. *The Playworld of Sanskrit Drama.* Delhi: Motilal Banarsidass.

Greenough, Paul, 1996. "Nation, Economy and Tradition Displayed: The Indian Crafts Museum", in Carol Brekenridge (ed.), *Consuming Modernity: Public Culture in Contemporary India*. Delhi: Oxford University Press (216-248).

Greimas, A. J., 1971, "The Interpretation of Myth: Theory and Practice", in Elli K. Maranda (ed.), *Structural Analysis of Oral Tradition.* Philadelphia: University of Pensylvania (81-121).

Guha, Ranajit, 1983. *Elementary Aspects of Peasant Insurgency in Colonial India*. Delhi: Oxford University Press.

Guha-Thakurta, Tapati, 1992. *The Making of a New 'Indian' Art. Artists, Aesthetics and Nationalism in Bengal 1850-1920.* Cambridge: Cambridge University Press.

Handoo, Jawaharlal, 2004. "The Palace Paradigm: Historical Space and Folklore", in M.D. Muthukumaraswamy and Molly Kaushal (eds.), *Folklore, Public Sphere and Civil Society.* New Delhi & Chennai: Indira Gandhi National Centre for the Arts and National Folklore Support Centre (57-65).

Haque, Abu Saeed Zahurul, 1976. *Folklore and Nationalism in Rabindranath Tagore.* Dhaka: Bangla Academy.

Hardy, Friedhelm, 1983. *Viraha Bhakti: The Early History of Krishna Devotion in South India.* Delhi: Oxford University Press.

Hoffman, John and Arthur van Emelen, 1965. *Encyclopedia Mundarica.* Vol. II. Patna: Government Printing.

Humes, Cynthia Ann, 1998. "Vindhyavasini/ Local Goddess yet Great Goddess", in John Stratton Hawley and Donna Marie Wulf (eds.), *Devi: Goddesses of India.* Delhi: Motilal Banarsidass (49-76).

Hunt, Alan and Gary Wickham, 1994. *Foucault and Law: Towards a Sociology of Law as Governance*. London: Pluto Press.

Joas, Hans, 1985. *G. H. Mead: A Contemporary Re-Examination of his Thought.* Cambridge: Polity Press.

Kar,Tapan, 1994. *Asamanya Manbhum.* Calcutta: Ananda Publishers.

Kerketta, Jonas, 1987. *Evangelization of the Adivasis in Assam: A Study in Historical and Theological Perspective* (Unpublished M. Th. Dissertation. Sacred Heart Theological College, Shillong).

Kirshenblatt-Gimblett, Barbara, 1998. "Folklore's Crisis", *Journal of American Folklore.* Vol. III (281-327).

Levi Strauss, Claude, 1970. *The Raw and the Cooked.* London: Jonathan Cape.

Mahato, Bankim, 1978. "Chho Naach: Ekti Shomikha", *Chhatrak.* Vol. III. (205-213).

Mahato, Pashupati Prasad, 1987. *The Performing Arts of Jharkhand.* Calcutta: B.B. Prakashan

——, 2001. *Jharkhander Hara-Mitan (Kheroal) Samajik Sabhyata. Shilpa Chetona o Jibanrausbodh.* Calcutta: Ashok Chakravarti.

Malamoud, Charles, 1989. "Indian Speculations about the Sex of the Sacrifice", in Michel Feher, Ramona Naddaff and Nadia Tazi (eds.), *Fragments for a History of the Human Body.* Part I. New York: Zone (18-74).

Manuel, Peter, 1989. *Thumri in History and Stylistic Perspectives.* Delhi: Motilal Banarsidass.

Marriott, Mckim, 1955. "Little Communities in an Indigenous Civilization", in Mckim Marriott (ed.), *India's Villages.* Chicago: University of Chicago Press (171-222).

Mauss, Marcel, 1972. *A General Theory of Magic.* London: Routledge & Kegan Paul.

McDaniel, June, 2003. *Making Virtuous Daughters and Wives: An Introduction to Women's Brata Rituals in Bengali Folk Religion.* New York: State University of New York Press.

McDermott, Rachel Fell, 2001. *Singing to the Goddess: Poems to Kali and Uma from Bengal.* New York: Oxford University Press.

Minz, Nirmal, 1997. *Rise Up, My People, and Claim the Promise: The Gospel among the Tribes of India.* Delhi: Indian Society for Promoting Christian Knowledge.

Monier-Williams, Monier, 1899. *A Sanskrit-English Dictionary.* Oxford: Clarendon Press.

Morinis, E. A., 1982. "Baba Taraknath: A Case of Continuity and Development in the Folk Tradition of West Bengal, India", *Asian Folklore Studies.* Vol. 41 (1) (67-81).

Motz, Marilyn, 1998. "The Practice of Belief", *The Journal of American Folklore.* Vol. III (339-355).

Naregal, Veena, 2001. *Language Politics, Elites and the Public Sphere.* Delhi: Permanent Black.

Natih, Susan, 1985. *Chhau Diaries.* Devon: Dartington College of Arts.

Orsini, Francesca, 2002. *The Hindi Public Sphere 1920-1940. Language and Literature in the Age of Nationalism.* Delhi: Oxford University Press.

Piatigorsky, Alexander, 1993. *Mythological Deliberations. Lectures on the Phenomenology of Myth.* London: School of Oriental and African Studies.

Pradhan, Sudhi, 1979. *Marxist Cultural Movements in India: Chronicals and Documents.* Vol. I (1936-1947). Calcutta: Pustak Bipani.

Propp, Vladimir, 1984. *Theory and History of Folklore.* Manchester: Manchester University Press.

Quinn, Malcom, 1994. *Swastika: Constructing the Symbol.* London: Routledge.

Radhakrishna, Meena, 2001. *Dishonoured by History. 'Criminal Tribes' and British Colonial policy.* Delhi: Orient Longman.

Raghavan, V., 1980. *The Ramayana Tradition in Asia.* Delhi: Sahitya Akademi.

Raheja, Gloria Goodwin and Ann Grodzins Gold, 1996. *Listen to the Heron's Words: Reimagining Gender and Kinship in North India.* Delhi: Oxford University Press.

Rao, Vidya, 2000. "Thumri as Feminine Voice", in Nivedita Menon (ed.), *Gender and Politics in India.* Delhi: Oxford University Press (475-491).

Rappaport, Joanne, 1994. *Cumbe Reborn: An Andean Ethnography of History.* Chicago: University of Chicago Press.

Redfield, Robert, 1955. *Peasant Society and Culture.* Chicago: University of Chicago Press.

Roy, Nityananda, 1972. "Tushu o Tushu Gaan", *Chhatrak* (114-147).

Roychaudhury, Mahua, 1996. "Banglar Loknritto ar Goudiyo Nritto", *Lokshruti,* Vol. 12 (89-120).

Samaddar, Shekhar, 2004. "Shundorer Nidhon: Bastobbe o Natye", *Desh.* 17th March (85).

Sanyal, Hiteshranjan, 2004. *Selected Writings.* Calcutta: Centre for Archaelogical Research and Training, Eastern India.

Sarkar, Benoy Kumar, 1941. *The Folk–Element in Hindu Culture.* Delhi: Munshiram Manoharlal (1st published in 1916).

——, 1985. *The Positive Background of Hindu Sociology.* Delhi: Motilal Banarsidass (1st published in 1937).

Sarkar, Sumit, 1973. *The Swadeshi Movement in Bengal.* (1903-1908) Delhi: Peoples' Publishing House.

Sarkar, Tanika, 1985. "Jitu Santhal's Movement in Malda, 1924-1932: A Study in Tribal Protest", in Ranajit Guha (ed.), *Subaltern Studies IV. Writings on South Asian History and Society.* Delhi: Oxford University Press (136-164).

——, 1999. *Words to Win. The Making of Amar Jibon: A Modern Autobiography.* Delhi: Kali.

——, 2001. *Hindu Wife, Hindu Nation.* Delhi: Permanent Black.

Schechner, Richard, 1983. *Performative Circumstances from the Avant Garde to Ramlila.* Calcutta: Seagull Books

Schutz, Alfred and Thomas Luckman, 1973. *The Structures of the Life-World.* Evanston: Northwestern University Press.

Sen, Dinesh Chandra, 1985. *The Folk Literature of Bengal.* Delhi: B.R. Publishing Corporation (1st published in 1920).

——, 1986. *History of Bengali Language and Literature.* Delhi: Gyan Publishing House (lectures delivered in Calcutta University, January-April 1909).

Sen, Sukumar, 1960. *History of Bengali Literature.* Delhi: Sahitya Akademi.

Sen Gupta, Sankar, 1965. *Folklorists of Bengal. Life-Sketches and Bibliographical Notes.* Calcutta: Indian Publishers.

Singh, Mani Shekhar, 2007. "Religious Iconography, Violence and The Making of a Series", *Domains* (III) (38-65).

Sinha, Surajit, 1957. "Tribal Culture in Peninsular India as a Dimension of the Little Tradition in the Study of Indian Civilization: A Preliminary Statement", *Man in India*. Vol. 37 (93-118).

——, 1995. "State Formation and Rajput Myth in Tribal Central India", in Hermann Kulke (ed.), *The State in India. 1000-1700*. Delhi: Oxford University Press (304-342) (1st presented as the 49th Indian Science Congress in Cuttack in 1962).

——, n.d. "Vaishnava Influences on a Tribal Culture" (unpublished paper).

Sinha, Shanti, 1997. *Lok Sangeet Sangraha: Jhumur*. Calcutta: Paschim Rajya Sangeet Akademi.

——, 1974. (1405 B.S.). *Tushu*. Calcutta: Loksanskriti and Adivasi Sanskriti Kendra.

Sontheimer, Gunther-Dietz, 1997. *King of Hunters, Warriors and Shepherds. Essays on Khandoba* (Anne Feldhaus, Aditya Malik and Heidrun Bruckner eds.). Delhi: IGNCA & Manohar.

——, 1995. "The Erosion of Folk Religion in Modern India: Some Points for Deliberation", in Vasudha Dalmia and Henri von Stietencron (eds.), *Representing Hinduism: The Construction of Religious Traditions and National Identity*. Delhi: Sage (389-400).

Swapna Sundari, 2005. *The World of Kuchipudi Dance*. Delhi: Shubhi Publications.

Tagore, Abanindranath, 1919. (1350 B.S.), *Banglar Broto*. Shantiniketan: Vishwabharati.

Trautmann, Thomas R., 1997. *Aryans and British India*. Delhi: Vistaar Publications.

Trawick, Margaret, 1990. "Untouchability and the Fear of Death in a Tamil Song", in C. A. Lutz and Lila Abu-Lugod (eds.), *Language and Politics of Emotion*. Cambridge: Cambridge University Press (186-206).

van den Bogaert, Michael, 1993. "Communication, Community and Tribals", *Sevartham*. Vol. 3 (43-55).

van Exem, A., 1982. *The Religious System of the Munda Tribe: An Essay in Religious Anthropology*. St. Augustin 1: Haus Volker and Kulturen.

Warner, Michael, 2002. "Publics and Counter Publics", *Public Culture* 14 (1) (49-90).

Warshaver, Gerald, 1991. "On Postmodern Folklore", *Western Folklore*. Vol. 50 (3), (219-229).

Xaxa, Virginius, 2003. "Tribes in India", in Veena Das (ed.), *The Oxford India Companion to Sociology and Social Anthropology*. Delhi: Oxford University Press (368-372).

Author Index

Subject Index